Dean E. Arnold

Pottery Technology

See p. vii

D0024001

Pottery Technology

Ideas and Approaches

EDITED BY

Gordon Bronitsky

Westview Press
BOULDER, SAN FRANCISCO, & LONDON

Westview Special Studies in Archaeological Research

This Westview softcover edition is printed on acid-free paper and bound in softcovers that carry the highest rating of the National Association of State Textbook Administrators, in consultation with the Association of American Publishers and the Book Manufacturers' Institute.

All rights reserved. No part of this publication may be reproduced or transmitted in any form or by any means, electronic or mechanical, including photocopy, recording, or any information storage and retrieval system, without permission in writing from the publisher.

Copyright © 1989 by Westview Press, Inc.

Published in 1989 in the United States of America by Westview Press, Inc., 5500 Central Avenue, Boulder, Colorado 80301, and in the United Kingdom by Westview Press, Inc., 13 Brunswick Centre, London WC1N 1AF, England

Library of Congress Cataloging-in-Publication Data
Pottery technology : ideas and approaches / edited by Gordon
  Bronitsky.
    p. cm. — (Westview special studies in archaeological
research)
  ISBN 0-8133-7478-2
  1. Pottery. 2. Archaeology—Methodology. I. Bronitsky, Gordon.
II. Series.
CC79.5.P6P68 1989
730.1′028′5—dc19   87-34525
                                                                        CIP

Printed and bound in the United States of America

♾ The paper used in this publication meets the requirements of the American National
Standard for Permanence of Paper for Printed Library Materials Z39.48-1984.

10   9   8   7   6   5   4   3   2   1

Contents

PART THREE
CERAMIC TECHNOLOGY
AND SOCIOECONOMIC SYSTEMS

PART FOUR
CERAMIC ANALYSIS AND THE
STUDY OF FORMATION PROCESSES

PART FIVE
THE ARCHAEOLOGIST AND THE
ARCHAEOMETRICIAN: LARGER QUESTIONS

Acknowledgments

This volume is the end result of many years of work. Cindy Adams saw it through to the finish—no easy task. I am grateful indeed for the patience of all contributors, and I especially appreciate the financial contributions from Michael Schiffer, Dwight Wallace and Terry Childs. Finally, three archaeologists have continued to show me that the archaeometric study of ceramics means more than provenience studies and dating. For hours of discussion and argument, for moral support and for friendship in the truest sense of the word, I dedicate this volume to Peter McKenna, Michael Schiffer and Dean Arnold.

Gordon Bronitsky

Thanks for friendship + great conversation — but no gerunds!

Gordon

1

Introduction

Gordon Bronitsky

Anthropology and Archaeology Consultant,
Albuquerque, New Mexico

Ceramic technology has been defined as the 'investigation of the physical, mineralogical and chemical properties of ceramic materials by means of precise, objective and replicable standards' (Rice 1977:225). Archaeologists have been aware of the existence of a variety of measures for mineralogical and chemical characterization of ceramics and their potential utility in archaeological research at least since the pioneering work of Shepard (1957; see Matson 1952 for a review of earlier studies). Characterization describes those features of composition and structure of a material which are important for the preparation of a product, the study of its properties, or its ultimate uses (Hench 1971:1).

However, until recently, little use has been made of such measures beyond an increased emphasis on analysis of materials for provenance studies as techniques have become available (e.g., neutron activation analysis). These new techniques fit in well with traditional archaeological concerns with trade and cultural contact. The neglect of the physical aspects of ceramic characterization has not stemmed from the inconclusiveness or complexity of the methods but rather from the absence of theoretical problems for which such data would be relevant (see Shepard 1966). Most ceramic studies have concentrated on the construction of descriptive typologies as a basis for the establishment of temporal frameworks and cultural boundaries. For such purposes, stylistic attributes have often been most easily analyzed and assumed to be most sensitive to temporal and social variability (but see S. Plog 1980 for a general critique of this assumption). Accordingly, physical characterization studies of a ceramic collection in such a case would simply provide an additional data appendix which would be both costly and relatively meaningless.

Since the early 1970's, there has been an upsurge of interest in questions of ceramic technology. In large part, this renewed interest has occurred in the context of investigations of the socioeconomic context of production. Why were certain materials chosen by the potter? What functions did different vessels serve? How did functions and materials change through time? For example, recent archaeological research has suggested that changes in ceramic technology such as shifts in types, grades or amounts of temper have ramifications beyond simple changes in cultural preferences. In the Midwest, Braun (1983) has demonstrated a relationship between shifts in types of temper and increasing dependence on maize, due to physical properties of shell temper which enabled vessels to better withstand the repeated heating and cooling cycles needed to cook maize-based stews and gruels. Decreasing thickness of vessel walls through time was another mechanism potters employed to further reduce leakage due to thermal shock. Other research (Steponaitis 1983) has examined the relationship between size grades of temper and vessel resistance to mechanical stress and thermal shock. Still other work has pointed out the link between changes in physical characteristics of ceramics and the rise of specialized social and production systems (e.g., Bronitsky 1978; Rice 1981; Rye 1981).

This volume brings together an impressive array of studies of ceramic technology. The broad areal coverage and range of analytical techniques employed testify to a rapidly growing interest in the study of ceramic technology in a socioeconomic context. Several of the papers deal with the choices and problems faced by potters in the production process (e.g., papers by Matson, Wallace, van As). Others explore a range of techniques to refine our knowledge of the production processes themselves (e.g., papers by Stoltman, Johnston, Kaiser and Lucius). Others look at the ways in which changes in ceramic technology and function related to larger changes in social and economic systems (e.g., paper by Childs). The Upham and Plog paper is a more general review of the working relationships between archaeologists and archaeometricians, based on their own experience and data. As such, it provides a good transition to the review articles that follow.

The review articles constitute general appraisals of the analytical approaches used in the study of ceramic technology, the role of ceramic technology studies in the investigation of socioeconomic systems, and a general historical overview of such studies. As such, they place the other papers in the volume in the context of a new wave of cooperation between archaeologists and materials scientists in the study of the potters and consumers behind the myriad sherds of the archaeological record.

References Cited

Braun, D. "Pots as Tools." in *Archaeological Hammers and Theories,* edited by A. Keene and J. Moore. New York: Academic Press, pp. 107–134, 1983.

Bronitsky, G. "Postclassic Maya Plainware Ceramics: Measures of Homogeneity." in *Papers on the Economy and Architecture of the Ancient Maya,* edited by R. Sidrys. UCLA Institute of Archaeology Monograph, 8:142–154, 1978.

Hench, L. "Introduction to the Characterization of Ceramics." in *Characterization of Ceramics,* edited by L. Hench and R. Gould. New York: Marcel Dekker, pp. 1–5, 1971.

Matson, F. "Ceramic Technology as an Aid to Cultural Interpretation—Techniques and Problems." in *Essays on Archaeological Methods,* edited by J. Griffin. University of Michigan Museum of Anthropology, Anthropological Papers, 8:102–115, 1952.

Plog, S. *Stylistic Variation in Prehistoric Ceramics.* London: Cambridge University, 1980.

Rice, P. "Evolution of Specialized Pottery Production: A Trial Model." *Current Anthropology* 22(3):219–227, 1981.

Rye, O. *Pottery Technology: Principles and Reconstruction.* Washington, D.C.: Taraxacum, 1981.

Steponaitis, V. *Ceramics, Chronology and Community Patterns: An Archaeological Study of Moundville.* New York: Academic Press, 1983.

2

A Ceramics Manifesto

Gordon Bronitsky

Anthropology and Archaeology Consultant,
Albuquerque, New Mexico

Pots, pots everywhere—their broken remains are among the most widespread traces of human occupation. Archaeologists have long been aware of the utility of ceramic studies for reconstructing past human behavior. Most ceramic studies concentrate on the reconstruction of descriptive typologies in order to establish temporal sequences and cultural boundaries within a cultural-historical framework. For such purposes, stylistic attributes have often been assumed the most sensitive to temporal and social variability and the most easily analyzed (but see Plog 1980 for a critique of the assumptions inherent in this approach). As a result, stylistic studies have been an essential part of archaeological research since Sir Flinders Petrie.

However, archaeologists have also been interested in the functions of the pottery they excavate and the technology that produced them, an approach Braun (1983) has called the study of pots as tools. In the United States, such interest dates back at least to the pioneering work of Holmes (1903), who introduced such terms as *temper* and *surface finish* to the archaeological literature. The most common approach to the study of ceramic function and technology has been through ethnographic reviews of vessel form and stated use in order to derive functional correlates for further archeological testing (e.g., Ericson *et al.* 1971; Henrickson and McDonald 1983). At best, these measures are abstractions one step removed from the actual production and use of a pot. Form-function correlates are only one line of evidence that must be complemented by other approaches if ceramic function is to be inferred and understood.

In order to review these other approaches, it is necessary to present a number of basic materials science concepts and analytic approaches.

A material is simply anything that has a "characteristic identity recognizable by the two senses of sight and touch" (Tweeddale 1973:1). In an engineering and materials science sense, "material" is generally used as an abbreviated form of "material of construction" or "material of manufacture." In turn, materials science has been defined as the "generation and application of knowledge relating the composition, structure and processing of materials to their properties and uses" (Cohen 1980:xii). Most archaeologists are familiar with materials science analytic approaches in the study of artifact provenance, that is, the determination of geological origins of materials (after Freestone 1982). A diverse array of techniques has been employed toward this end, including neutron activation analysis, X-ray diffraction, X-ray fluorescence, atomic absorption spectroscopy, Mossbauer spectroscopy, and others. In materials science, such techniques fall into the category of characterization studies. *Characterization* refers to the differentiation and comparison of ceramic materials and fabrics in terms of their preparation and use (Freestone 1982:106). Archaeologists have known of such measures at least since the pioneering work of Shepard (1957; see Matson 1952 for a review of earlier studies). These techniques have been reviewed in detail elsewhere (e.g. Bishop, Rands, and Holley 1982; Drews 1976; Goffer 1980; Harbottle 1982; Peacock 1970; Wilson 1978) and will not be considered further here.

Two other spheres of materials science characterization studies are relevant in the study of ancient ceramic technology: (1) assessment of the relative efficacy of different materials in the manufacture of archaeological ceramics and (2) the contribution of different materials and techniques to vessel durability as measured through simulated-use techniques. Until recently, these function-related characterization measures have not found much actual application in archaeological research. This neglect has stemmed not from the inconclusiveness or complexity of the method but rather from a lack of emphasis on theoretical problems for which such data would be relevant (see Kingery 1980; Matson 1965:202, 1981; Rice 1982:4; Shepard 1966) and the lack of appropriate equipment in archaeological laboratories. Without relevant domains of inquiry to guide research, characterization studies of ceramic collections would simply provide an additional data appendix which would be both costly and meaningless.

Materials science analytic approaches have begun attracting archaeological interest as studies of the cultural context of production and use have grown—"ceramic ecology," to use Matson's (1965:202) term. At the level of the individual potter, the context includes the choices and problems encountered in production and the compromises made in materials in order to arrive at a finished product (after van der Leeuw 1976:393, 1984a:57). Understanding these choices requires more accurate assessment of the system of ceramic manufacture at hand and the existing knowledge system; the kinds of clay utilized, the reasons for their use, and the kinds of manipulations required to arrive at the final ceramic product.

Cultural norms as well as the properties and preliminary treatment of clay all affect the shape of the pot (Franken 1971:237; Kalsbeek 1969:73), which is, in turn, related to the skill of the potter and the uses for which the pot is intended. Did the potter mix clays well? Was the potter skilled in construction or are there numerous defects in the vessel? Was the vessel used to prepare or serve soup or nuts, gruel or greens? The shape can provide clues to use, and a number of analytic techniques can be used to assess the extent to which the ceramic fabric was suitable for a particular activity.

The uses of a pot are intimately related to the social environment of its maker and users. Materials science approaches can provide insights into the manner in which changes in ceramic technology and function related to larger changes in social and economic systems. Some archaeologists have argued against any direct linkage between social and ceramic change, using studies from such diverse regions as Nubia (Adams 1979), the historic Teotihuacaán valley (Charlton 1968) and Aymara Peru (Tschopik 1951). Such apparent lack of correlation may be due to (1) ceramic stability in situations where daily needs were well met by local pottery, (2) the use of time spans which are too long for measuring small-scale, constantly accumulating change, or (3) the use of analytic frameworks which are too general and impressionistic to measure such change (Rice 1984:272–273). A more productive approach to this problem would be an evaluation of the shifts in requirements for ceramic materials in relation to social and cultural changes in order to test the hypothesis that the level of ceramic technology responds to perceived needs (Kingery 1984; Rice 1984:174).

Further, materials science approaches can provide data on changes in standards of acceptable performance and the increasing skills of potters in meeting these standards through manipulation of ceramic materials (after Rice 1981:222–223; van der Leeuw 1984b:743). The development of such standards is an integral part of the rise of specialized production, the development of what Pye (1968:4) has called the "workmanship of certainty," in which the quality of the final product is predetermined. The use of materials science analytic approaches can permit an assessment of the range of variation for a number of behaviorally relevant physical properties such as porosity, permeability, and vessel strength. As these studies are incorporated into investigations of the socioeconomic context of production, we can begin to approach an understanding of cultural change and evolution. For example, participation in a market economy has been linked to the deterioration of a subsistence economy due to environmental degradation. One aspect of this degradation is arroyo-cutting, which often exposes new clay sources as the traditional economy declines, providing a new or greatly expanded means of subsistence (Arnold 1978; Ellen and Glover 1974; Gross *et al.* 1979). In turn, market demands spur innovations in styles and production techniques (Foster 1961; Papousek 1984). An evaluation of changes in production technology and finished product can elucidate the links among these factors in cultural change.

The study of "pots as tools" may begin with a seemingly simple and specific question, such as, Why do potters add temper to clay? However, the search for an answer may require that archaeologists wander rather far afield from traditional archaeological knowledge domains into materials testing, engineering, and more. Nonetheless, the primary goal remains an understanding of human behavior, not the physical behavior of inert composites. The latter is the only means by which the former can be understood.

Searching for answers to questions about pottery technology will benefit archaeologists at several levels. At the materials level, the research will constitute a rigorous assessment of ceramic durability in several physicomechanical dimensions for a variety of materials and a variety of wares. This assessment will permit an evaluation of the extent to which vessel function played a role in temper selection. Such assessment is part of a growing concern with the broader socioeconomic context of the potter and the uses of pots as tools (Braun 1983). The interrelated mechanical analysis of clays and vessels can ultimately help us understand the choices and problems the potter faced. In so doing, more accurate assessments of ceramic technology and reconstruction of the potter's craft can be made, as we realize what kinds of clay were utilized, why they were chosen, and the kinds of manipulation required to arrive at the final product.

Answering these questions will require efforts from many disciplines in order to relate analytic approaches designed for commercial ceramics to archaeological pots and to link laboratory studies with real-world sherds, vessels, and potters (see Bronitsky 1986 for a fuller review of this issue). Ironically, it will require the efforts of a variety of "high tech" specialists, working in conjunction with archaeologists, to begin to understand the technical dilemmas, solutions and expertise of so-called "primitive" potters.

References Cited

Adams, W.Y. "On the Argument from Ceramics to History: A Challenge Based on Evidence from Medieval Nubia." *Current Anthropology.* 20(4):727–744, 1979.

Arnold, D. "Ceramic Variability, Environment and Culture History among the Pokom in the Valley of Guatemala." in *The Spatial Organization of Culture,* edited by I. Hodder. London: Duckworth, pp. 39–59, 1978.

Bishop, R., Harbottle, G., and Sayre, E. "Chemical and Mathematical Procedures Employed in the Maya Fine Paste Ceramics Project." in *Excavations at Seibal, No. 2: Analyses of Fine Paste Ceramics,* edited by J. Sabloff. *Peabody Museum Memoirs* 15(2):272–282, 1982.

Braun, D. "Pots as Tools." in *Archaeological Hammers and Theories,* edited by A. Keene and J. Moore. New York: Academic Press, pp. 107–134, 1983.

Bronitsky, G. "The Use of Materials Science Techniques in the Study of Pottery Construction and Use." in *Advances in Archaeological Method and Theory,* Vol. 9, edited by M. Schiffer. New York: Academic Press, pp. 209–276, 1986.

Charlton, T.H. "Post-Conquest Aztec Ceramics: Implications for Archaeological Interpretation." *Flordia Anthropologist.* 21:96–101, 1968.

Cohen, M. "Materials in Human Affairs." in *Elements of Materials Science and Engineering (Fourth Edition),* edited by L.H. Van Vlack. Reading, Massachusetts: Addison-Wesley, pp. vii–xix, 1980.

Drews, G. "Geochemische Klassifizierung und Lokalisierung keramischen Bodenfunde." *Festschrift Hundt,* Teil 3, pp. 229–249. *Jahrbuch des Römisch-Germanischen Zentralmuseums.* 23–24, Mainz, 1976.

Ellen, R., and Glover, J. "Pottery Manufacture and Trade in the Central Moluccas, Indonesia: The Modern Situation and the Historial Implications." *Man.* (n.s.) 9:353–379, 1974.

Ericson, J., Read, D., and Burke, C. "Research Design: The Relationships between the Primary Functions and the Physical Properties of Ceramic Vessels and their Implications for Ceramic Distribution on an Archaeological Site. *Anthropology UCLA.* 3(2):84–95, 1971.

Foster, R. "The Sociology of Pottery: Questions and Hypotheses Arising from Contemporary Mexican Work." in *Ceramics and Man,* edited by F. Matson. Chicago: Aldine, pp. 43–61, 1961.

Franken, H.J. "Analysis of Methods of Potmaking in Archaeology." *Harvard Theological Review.* 64:227–255, 1971.

Freestone, I. "Applications and Potential of Electron Probe Microanalysis in Technology and Provenance Investigations of Ancient Ceramics. *Archaeometry.* 27(1):3–16, 1982.

Goffer, Z. *Archaeological Chemistry: A Sourcebook on the Applications of Chemistry to Archaeology.* New York: Wiley, 1980.

Gross, D., Eiten, G., Flowers, N., Leoi, F., Ritter, M., and Werner, D. "Ecology and Acculturation among Native Peoples of Central Brazil. *Science.* 206(4422): 1043–1050, 1979.

Harbottle, G. "Provenance Studies using Neutron Activation Analysis: The Role of Standardization." in *Archaeological Ceramics*, edited by J. Olin and A. Franklin. Washington, D.C.: Smithsonian Institution, pp. 67–77, 1982.

Henrickson, E., and McDonald, M. "Ceramic Form and Function: An Ethnographic Search and an Archaeological Problem." *American Anthropologist*. 85(3):630–643, 1983.

Holmes, W. "Aboriginal Pottery of the Eastern United States." *Bureau of American Ethnology, Twentieth Annual Report*. Washington, D.C.: Smithsonian Institution, pp. 1–237, 1903.

Kalsbeek, J. "A systematic Approach to the Study of the Iron Age Pottery." in *Excavations at Tell Deir 'Alla*, by H.J. Franken. Leiden: E.J. Brill, pp. 73–80, 1969.

Kingery, W. "Social Needs and Ceramic Technology." *Bulletin of the American Ceramic Society*. 59:598–600, 1980.

———. "Interactions of Ceramic Technology with Society." in *Pots and Potters: Current Approaches in Ceramic Archaeology*, edited by P. Rice. UCLA Institute of Archaeology Monograph, 24:171–178, 1984.

Matson, F. "The Contribution of Technical Ceramic Studies to American Archaeology." in *Prehistoric Pottery of the Eastern United States*, edited by J. Griffin. Papers of the Museum of Anthropology of the University of Michigan No. 2 Ann Arbor, 1952.

———. "Ceramic Ecology: An Approach to the Study of Early Cultures of the Near East." in *Ceramics and Man*, edited by F. Matson. Chicago: Aldine, pp. 202–217, 1965.

———. "Archaeological Ceramics and the Physical Sciences: Problem Definition and Results." *Journal of Field Archaeology*. 8(4):448–456, 1981.

Papousek, D. "Pots and People in Los Pueblos: The Social and Economic Organization of Pottery." in *The Many Dimensions of Pottery*, edited by S. Van der Leeuw and A. Pritchard. Amsterdam: University of Amsterdam, pp. 465–519, 1984.

Peacock, D. "The Scientific Analysis of Ancient Ceramics: A Review." *World Archaeology*. 1(3):375–389, 1970.

Plog, S. *Stylistic Variation in Prehistoric Ceramics*. London: Cambridge University, 1980.

Pye, D. *The Nature and Art of Workmanship*. London: Cambridge University, 1968.

Rice, P. "Evolution of Specialized Pottery Production: A Trial Model. *Current Anthropology*. 22(3):219–227, 1981.

———. "Pottery Production, Pottery Classification, and the Role of Physicochemical Analyses."in *Archaeological Ceramics*, edited by J. Olin and A. Franklin. Washington, D.C.: Smithsonian Institution, pp. 47–56, 1982.

———. "Change and Conservatism in Pottery-Producing Systems." in *The Many Dimensions of Pottery*, edited by S. van der Leeuw and A. Pritchard. Amsterdam: University of Amsterdam, pp. 231–287, 1984.

Shepard, A. "Ceramics for the Archaeologist." *Carnegie Institution of Washington Publication*. No. 609, 1957.

———. "Problems in Pottery Study." *American Antiquity*. 31(6):870–871, 1966.

Tschopik, H. "An Andean Ceramic Tradition in Historical Perspective." *American Antiquity.* 15:196–218, 1951.

Tweeddale, J. *Materials Technology,* Vol. 1, "The Nature of Materials." London: Butterworth, 1973.

van der Leeuw, S. *Studies in the Technology of Ancient Pottery.* Unpublished PhD dissertation, University of Amsterdam, 1976.

————. "Dust to Dust: A Transformation View of the Ceramic Cycle." in *The Many Dimensions of Pottery,* edited by S. van der Leeuw and A. Pritchard. Amsterdam: University of Amsterdam, pp. 707–773, 1984a.

————. "Pottery Manufacture: Some Complications for the Study of Trade." in *Pots and Potters: Current Approaches in Ceramic Archaeology,* edited by P. Rice. UCLA Institute of Archaeology Monograph 24:55–70, 1984b.

Wilson, A. "Elemental Analysis of Pottery in the Study of its Provenance: A Review." *Journal of Archaeological Science.* 5:291–236, 1978.

PART ONE

Ceramic Production: The Potter's Perspective

3

Shell-Tempered Pottery and the Fort Ancient Potter

Frederick R. Matson

Department of Anthropology, Pennsylvania State University

The Shell Tempering of Pottery

Some years ago I deserted my laboratory studies of shell-tempered pottery, particularly those of the Fort Ancient culture of southwestern Ohio and adjoining regions, so as to complete my doctoral dissertation on Near Eastern pottery. In returning now to these earlier studies and amplifying them, I approach this work with a somewhat different point of view than that which I had in 1939. This is encouraging! At that time I was concerned primarily with the measurement of the physical and mineralogical properties of ancient pottery. Now, having had the opportunity to observe and talk with potters still working in villages in several parts of the world, I am far more interested in examining sherds for clues relating to man, their maker and user, than in defining the properties of the clay that were selected, and at times tempered, with strange inclusions.

The addition of shell, rock or other materials to clays by potters has been ably discussed by Owen Rye. Recently David Braun effectively summarized many of the physical aspects of the inclusion of rock in Woodland pottery with respect to mechanical and thermal stress. Vincas Steponaitis presented a good paper at the Ceramics and Man II conference in which he reported on his testings of coarse and fine shell-tempered pottery from Moundsville, Alabama, suggesting that the shell size used by the potters was a function of the vessels that were being built. Our chairman has just given us a fine example of replicative studies of tempering materials versus impact and thermal shock resistance. These and other stimulating approaches, when tempered by closer collaboration with ceramic engineers, are welcome. The effect of the curvature of the

15

sherd walls and their thickness on the properties measured, as well as structural inhomogeneities in the bodies, must be accounted for when one attempts to explain why the vessels served their makers and users in a satisfactory manner. Today I should like to focus on the additions of calcined shell to clays as a means of preventing the clay from cracking badly while the vessel is being formed. I would then like to report briefly on some of my continuing studies of Fort Ancient pottery.

A problem which all potters face is the cracking of the plastic clay while the hand-made pot is being shaped. This problem is reduced in Afghanistan by the addition of cattail seeds whose fine surrounding filaments help bind the clay aggregates together. Other peoples have used straw, dung, feathers or, of course, sand or crushed rock in the paste. When the vessel walls are compacted during and after forming by the use of a paddle and anvil, for instance, a sturdy body can be produced. But the exact quantity and even the nature of the inclusions in the paste can vary daily within one household, depending upon many obvious factors. A skilled potter is much like a cook, and can improvise, using approximate quantities of ingredients and working "by the feel." However, the enumeration of such factors is another and best deferred story. I mention this obvious problem of local variability to suggest that detailed analysis of one or two sherds may produce suggestive results of value in training the investigator, but they can hardly serve to characterize the wares of a pottery-producing community. They are but preparation for such studies. There are great opportunities for more culturally productive technological projects today at several of the major excavations, and I trust that they are being pursued.

The idea of making pottery from the local clays near a site and the tempering materials recognized in the potsherds is not new. Frank H. Cushing, remembered for his pioneer work in the American Southwest and at Key Marco, Florida, collected sherds on the Canadian shore of Lake Erie, opposite Buffalo, ninety years ago, and noted that "the paste was charged with a tempering material of either calcined or pulverized stone (usually granite) or of burnt shells, or of both." He calcined shells and rocks separately and used them in his experiments reported in the long-forgotten article, "The Germ of Shoreland Pottery." He notes the cement-like hardening of the plastic tempered body, a point that I suggested as a desirable property resulting from the inclusion of calcined shell in bodies. His paper is well worth reading. Griffin and Angell experimented with the use of uncalcined shell as tempering material while at the Michigan Fresh Air Camp in 1933. Byers and Johnson tested the shells available on Martha's Vineyard in 1940, using a blowtorch to calcine the shells. Holmes, in his monumental report on "The Aboriginal Pottery of the Eastern United States" reports that DuPratz, in his Louisiana studies published in 1758, notes that the Indians tempered their pottery with ground shell. He missed a point, however, for he went on to say in Holmes' translation, "However, I would not advise the use of those shells for this purpose, because by nature they crack when exposed to fire."

That is exactly the point. Shells are composed of the minerals calcite and aragonite that expand from three to five times in length when heated to 80° Centigrade with shattering results. I have recently heated clam shells in my electric furnace, and found that observable cracks occurred at 200°C. (750°F.), and at 350° and 400°C. They were extensively cracked. When the hot shells were then immersed in water, they were destroyed. Crushing shells remaining after an Indian clambake in which steam was prevalent (as cited by Parmalee and Klippel), would be a simple procedure. We have laboratory studies under way in which shell calcined at several temperatures and then water-quenched is added to clay in varying amounts and grain sizes. The workability of the resulting pastes is then subjectively assessed. The next step would be to enlist the evaluative skills of a potter. The practical aspect of this approach would be to collect shells at riverain sites, experiment with their calcination, perhaps with clambakes, and then incorporate the calcined crushed materials in the clays available near the site that have been identified as possible raw materials used by the ancient potters. This study should proceed in conjunction with the field sorting of the shell-tempered sherds and an assessment of the amount and size of the shell included in them with respect to other variables of interest to the investigators.

In concluding this portion of the paper, I should like to again emphasize the need to keep in mind the practical aspects of the use of tempering materials such as shell. They may well serve their major role in helping provide the potter with a good workable paste with which to form vessels, one that hardens or "sets up" quickly, and one that is sufficiently porous so that the pots can dry adequately before being fired. The role of the inclusions in aiding the successful firing of the ware and in providing sturdy vessels for use may be irrelevant or even negative in its influence!

I should now like to report on laboratory and field studies of pottery from the Anderson Focus at Fort Ancient, Ohio, in terms of some of the raw materials available at the site and their relationship to the sherds studied. Exhaustive numerical detail will be avoided in this presentation. We are concerned with the potter at work.

This paper is an expression of my appreciation of the always stimulating and even controversial influence of Jimmy Griffin, who first interested me in the sherds of Fort Ancient.

The Potter at Fort Ancient

Abstract

Sherds from the village and fort areas at Fort Ancient, Ohio, on the Little Miami River in Warren County, Southwestern Ohio, have been published in considerable detail by Griffin (1943). The technological examination of some of the pottery from Fort Ancient and associated sites was done some years ago, but the information has remained in my files. In this paper the data obtained in the laboratory from the detailed study of the physical properties of some sherds and clays from the Anderson Focus at Fort Ancient will be used in evaluating the problems and success of the potters who made the wares.

The invitation to prepare a paper for this book presents me with the opportunity to publish data that were to have been included in Jimmy Griffin's landmark book, *The Fort Ancient Aspect.* An historical overview of ceramic studies and interests at the University of Michigan's Museum of Anthropology which began about fifty years ago and my changing ceramic interests since I first began work there in 1934 may help place these notes in perspective.

Ceramic studies were encouraged at Michigan, probably because of the interests of the Director of the Museum of Anthropology, the late Carl E. Guthe. He had excavated and collected Chinese wares in Philippine caves in the early 1920s, published the pioneer study of *Pueblo Pottery Making* in 1925, established the Ceramic Repository for the Eastern United States (which he described in a mimeographed invitation from the Museum to prospective donors of sherds in 1927), published a paper on *A Method of Ceramic Description* (1927) which was revised to serve as the first section of *Standards of Pottery Description* published in 1934 by his colleague, Benjamin March, who was interested in the study of Chinese ceramics. In addition, Guthe appointed Griffin as the Fellow in Aboriginal North American Ceramics. The first publication of the Ceramic Repository was Griffin's *An Analysis of the Fort Ancient Culture* in 1935.

I came to Michigan in the fall of 1934 as a University Fellow, working with the Ceramic Repository collections influenced in my approach by my undergraduate training as a Ceramic Engineer. The sherd collections from Fort Ancient, Oregonia, Feurt, Baum, Gartner, Madisonville and Fox Farm were in the collections that the Ceramic Repository had obtained, doubtless through Griffin's efforts, from the keepers of the major deposits of the excavated materials. I began studying and analyzing sherds from these sites of the Fort Ancient Aspect. In April, 1938, Jimmy Griffin organized a visit to Fort Ancient on which he was accompanied by Jim and Ethel Ford, George Neumann, John Cotter, George Quimby and myself. We visited the Fort Ancient and Oregonia sites with Cliff Anderson, the custodian of the Fort, as our guide. We were joined at the sites by Bill Haag, John Cotter, Dick Morgan and John Butler. Sherds were, of course, collected, and I obtained samples of three different clays at Fort Ancient. We then visited other sites in southwestern Ohio and northern Kentucky.

In November, 1938, a three-day conference was held at the Museum on "Archaeological Technology in Ceramics." This was made possible by a grant that Guthe obtained from the National Research Council. A brief report on the meeting was published by Shepard and Horton. Carl J. Engelder, Professor of Analytical Chemistry at the University of Pittsburgh, participated in the conference. During the conference, he strongly advised me to immediately defer work on all projects unrelated to the completion of my doctoral dissertation. In my laboratory notebook of that period after the last Fort Ancient entry in November, 1938, appeared the pencilled note: "Stopped work to spend full time on Ph.D. thesis so as to get my degree in June." My objective was achieved in June, 1939. In the spring of 1942, I returned to the study of the Fort Ancient pottery, but had to desist abruptly due to external demands we all faced in the national interests. Before leaving, I packed my materials in a series of cartons which were then stored for a decade or more. By then, my archaeological interests were firmly fixed in Near Eastern ceramic studies, and unpublished materials from other regions were not unpacked.

In returning now to the study of pottery from southwestern Ohio that was produced by agriculturists of the general Mississippian Culture, I approach it with a somewhat different point of view than that which I had in 1939. This is encouraging. At that time, I was concerned primarily with the measurement of the physical and mineralogical properties of ancient pottery. Now, having had the opportunity to observe and talk with potters still working in villages in several parts of the world, I am far more interested in examining sherds for clues relating to man, their maker, than in defining the properties of the clays which they selected and at times tempered. Therefore, I should like to present these data not as an analytical definition of a ware in terms of physical properties, but as indications of the problems resolved by the potters as they worked. Emphasis will be placed on the sherds from Fort Ancient itself. Very few of the sherds and my experimental test pieces are available to me for re-examination today, for they are on file in Ann Arbor and I have not found the necessary time to revisit them. Since but a small selection of the sherds excavated at Fort Ancient is available there, it would be desirable to continue similar studies at contemporary site excavations where the ceramic materials found are under methodological control. Recent studies by Dunnell and Rafferty, Hanson, Prufer and Shane point toward such possibilities in the redefined archaeological interests of the 1970s.

Clay Resources

The alluvial clay deposits on the flood plain of the Little Miami River below the limestone bluffs vary considerably in their sand and gravel content. The Illinoisan drift clays, often covered with later loess deposits, were available to the potters both on the valley floor and in the walls of the ravines which cut across it. Beneath these clays is a very impervious blue-gray fossiliferous shale. In the older geological literature, Brownocker (pp. 36–37), Flynn (pp. 164–171) and Leverett (pp. 282; 295) give useful information about the surface deposits and their drainage. Moorehead, the major excavator of Fort Ancient, provides several comments on the clays, for he knew the site intimately. He discusses the geological nature of the hill at the site (pp. 5–6), and the formation of the embankments of the fort (p. 10). In describing these embankments, he says, "In the earth below, the prevailing color is yellow, with streaks and patches of darker soil. This is probably due to the locality from which it was taken, some of it being loam gathered from the surface, while other portions came from a greater depth, and were, in consequence, yellow clay. Not a little blue clay appears. This the builders probably took from the limestone beds and from the hollows" (p. 31). On pp. 43–49, while discussing the later village site with which we are primarily concerned, he comments on river flooding, with sand and silt deposits building up during the last hundred years. Such flooding has become more frequent since lumbering operations have removed the trees and logs from the shores of the Little Miami River. In several places, he makes the point that the embankment clay is not easily penetrated by water, hence the structure has survived, despite continuing erosion in the general area. "Little streams have cut their channels through 50 to 100 feet of thin, horizontal layers of blue limestone, interstratified with indurated clay marl" (p. 72). "The yellow clay is found at depths of three feet in other parts of the moat" (p. 94).

Thus, the Fort Ancient potter at the village site had several kinds of clay available for her use, some tenaceous and dense, others sandy. (The term "sand" is used here in a very general sense with no implication of grain size.) The sherds that have been available for study clearly indicate variety in the ceramic resources used, for some vessels were formed of rather sandy clay and were relatively thick-walled (6–10 mm), while others were thin-walled vessels, 4–6 mm in thickness, and tempered with finely laminated shell. Many sherds had a paste containing fine sand and some shell. Were this a contemporary excavation with adequate control of all of the sherd material, it would be instructive to study the relationship between the kind of clay used and its texture, the addition of shell, the vessel sizes and their presumed use, and the areal and temporal distribution of the sherds at the site. Ceramic differences between the earlier occupants of the Fort and the later agriculturists at the village site in terms of clays selected, textural differences related to vessel size and shape, and firing treatment, as well as evidences of use, would be worth studying.

Three clays were sampled at Fort Ancient, and were labelled A, B, and C. Their physical and mineralogical characteristics can be briefly summarized without presenting all of the detailed information available and on file, as follows:

Source

    A. Yellow clay from within the walls of Fort Ancient sampled after 18″ of soil had been removed.

    B. Brown village site clay from the walls of the ravine.

    C. Fossiliferous shale exposed at the base of a ravine.

Color (in terms of the Munsell color system)

    Raw
    A. 2.5Y 7/4 Pale Yellow
    B. 10 YR 6/3 Pale Brown
    C. 5Y 7/1 Light Gray

    500° C.
    A. 7.5 YR 5.5/6 Strong Brown
    B. 7.5 YR 5.5/4 Light Brown
    C. 10YR 7/2 Light Gray

    800° C.
    A. 7.5YR 6.5/6 Reddish Yellow
    B. 10YR 6/3 Pale Brown
    C. 10YR 7/4 Very Pale Brown

Briquettes of each clay were fired to 500 and 800° C., holding each temperature for 30 minutes, to trace the color development in poorly and reasonably well-fired pottery.

Hardness (Mohs' scale)

The scratch hardness for the three clays was about the same. They had a hardness of slightly less than 2 when raw, and just less than 3 when fired to 900° C. for 30 minutes. The greatest difference in hardness within one firing increment was between 400° and 500° C. At this temperature range, much of the chemically combined water in the clay has disappeared, and the clay cannot again be made plastic.

Sieve Analysis

A. 2400 grams of clay were washed through a nest of seven standard sieves, 5, 7, 10, 14, 20, 35 and 60 mesh in screen size. 99.4% of the clay washed through the 20 mesh sieve.
B. Of the 933 grams in the sample, 99.4% of the clay washed through the 20 mesh sieve.

Mineralogical Constituents (identified from materials remaining on the sieves)

A. Limonitic sandstone grains dominant; some flint and quartz
B. Sandstone, often black and finely micaceous, was dominant; some flint and quartz and fossil fragments present.

pH (determined by Glenn A. Black)

A. 4.93 (acidic, which is normal for a sandy soil).
B. 7.25 (alkaline).
C. 8.05 (more strongly alkaline, due to shell and calcite inclusions).

Water of Plasticity

26% for all three clays. This measurement, determined for 4 to 7 test bars made from each clay, expresses the weight percentage of water needed, in terms of the dry weight of the clay, to make the clay plastic.

Linear Drying Shrinkage

A. 6.2% (range of 5.7–6.3% for 6 test bars).
B. 8.1% (range of 7.6–8.3% for 10 test bars).
C. 5.2% (range of 5.0–5.4% for 9 test bars).

The impervious clay underlying the site shrinks the least; the village site clay has the highest shrinkage.

Workability

All three clays could be easily worked when plastic and aged. Clay B, subjectively, seemed a bit less sticky and cracked less than did the other two, but all three clays could be used easily for pot making.

Summary

All three of the clays, as sampled, could have been used by the Fort Ancient potters. Clays with more sand in them could also have been employed successfully. It may be significant that the ravine clay from the village site had the highest shrinkage and the best workability. This is the clay, to be commented upon later, that was probably used for the manufacture of the shell-tempered pottery.

Shell-Tempered Clay Standards

In order to estimate·the amount of shell that was added to the clay by the potters, a series of standards was prepared from the village site clay B. Shell was first heated to cause it to laminate due to the great difference in the thermal expansion of calcite, the dominant mineral in shell. At the low temperatures that would be obtained in a hearth where mussels might be roasted, calcite will expand almost five times as much along its optical axis as it will be perpendicular to this axis. Hence shell is readily shattered when heated and can then be crushed easily. The shell, which was calcined at 300° C. for the test pieces was sieved, and the fraction used was that which passed through a 14 mesh sieve (1.4 mm openings) and was retained on the 20 mesh (0.84 mm openings). Clays tempered with 5, 10, 20, 30, 40, 50, and 60% shell by weight were prepared and formed into briquettes whose percent water of plasticity and percent linear drying shrinkage were measured. These were fired to 500° C. for one hour. After cooling, they were cut in half. One portion was ground smooth, but the other was left as a rough fractured surface. The series appears in Figure 3.3, and one has the impression of much more shell in a flat ground surface than in one which is roughly broken. Each briquette is one inch in width, so the relative scale can be estimated from the photograph. This illustration has appeared in two previous publications, but the test data relating to it have not heretofore been presented. Table 3.1 shows the changes in the two properties, measured as shell is increasingly added as tempering material to the village site clay. Even the paste containing 60% shell could still be worked.

As will be seen from Table 3.1, the shrinkage of the body progressively decreases with the addition of shell, and somewhat less water is required to render the paste plastic because, in part, less clay is present in the body. It will be noted that in the range from 10% to 30% shell, there is not much difference in the water needed. The shell thus reduces the shrinkage of the clay, but the body remains workable. Similar series of test pieces were prepared using crushed rock of two different grain size distributions as the tempering material, but the data will not be presented here. The test results for the rock tempered clay were quite similar to those for the shell series. It must be recognized that the data presented represent measurements on but one test piece for each stage, not averages of the results for several pieces, so the figures must be considered indicative, but by no means absolute.

The parallel laminae in the shell-tempered clay near the surfaces of the ground cross-section of the halved briquettes are well known to those who have worked with shell-tempered pottery; they certainly add strength to the body. It is no coincidence that shell-tempered ware is normally much thinner in wall thickness for the size of the vessel than is comparable ware made from shell-free or sandy clay. If one grinds the edge of a sherd smooth, preferably parallel to the vertical axis of the original vessel and at a right angle to the surface, the orientation of the laminae can be easily studied and clues as to the effective craftsmanship of the potters can be found. Occasionally, as several people have noted, one can recognize the juncture zone of two coils or slabs used in pot building from the disoriented swirl of the laminae and air holes.

Shell Content of Sherds

The standards just described were used to estimate the amount of shell that had been added to the paste of sherds from several foci of the Fort Ancient Aspect. When possible, a smoothly-ground surface was prepared, but a freshly broken fractured edge, using a small crescent wrench rather than pliers to snap off a small piece of the sherd from a protruding angle, could be compared with the unground standards. Sherds from the Anderson Focus at Fort Ancient, as well as Mill Grove, Madisonville, and Fox Farm sherds that were in the Ceramic Repository, were checked. In all 173 sherds were examined, and the results appear in Table 3.2.

Almost all of the sherds fall within the 10-30% estimated shell content, which agrees very well with the best working range for the standards, judging from their percent water of plasticity. It quickly became obvious as the sherds were examined that the amount of shell visible on the surface often bore no relation to the total amount of shell present.

In another approach to the estimation of the amount of shell present in sherds, nine Fort Ancient pieces were selected, and each sherd was broken in half. One portion had its edges carefully cleaned to remove any loose particles before the dry weights (4.5– 13 grams) of the test portions were determined. These prepared samples were then immersed in dilute hydrochloric acid for 46 hours. Three times during the immersion period, the container was gently heated to accelerate the decomposition of the shell. The pieces were then well washed, dried and weighed. It was found that they contained from 30% to 50.7% shell, with an average of 37.7%. Any siderite (iron carbonate) present, as well as hydrated iron compounds, would also be dissolved by this treatment, so the results are undoubtedly a little high.

A series of 14 sherds containing both sand and shell was also tested. Half of each piece was treated with dilute hydrochloric acid as in the previous series to determine the amount of shell present. This ranged from 9.4% to 18.8% with an average of 14.5%. The leached sherds were then subjected to a so-called rational analysis to remove the clay so as to isolate the sand. They were immersed in sulfuric acid for three days. During the acid treatment, the sherds were pulverized as much as possible with a glass rod to free more particles of clay. Heating the solution also helped in the decomposition of the clay. At the end of the treatment, the samples were washed several times until tests with litmus paper showed that they were acid-free. They were then dried and passed through a series of sieves. The residues retained on the sieves for five of the samples were accurately weighed. After sieving into sized fractions, the materials were gently rubbed with a rubber policeman in a mortar so as to pulverize the small clay lumps that had not dissolved in the acid. It was realized that such abrasion would further reduce the size of the more friable materials, particularly the sandstones, but it would have been too time-consuming to have separated all of the clay grains under a binocular microscope. However, for the fractions coarser than 20 mesh, such separation under a binocular microscope was carried out. Since the acid undoubtedly also attacked many of the minerals present, the final sieve residue results are certainly less than the amounts originally present. A little material from all five sherds was retained on the 14 mesh sieve (1.4–5.4%). Some also had materials on the 10 and 7 mesh sieves. (A 14 mesh sieve has 1.4mm openings; the 7 mesh, 2.8 mm.)

It was found that a summation of the weight of all the material coarser than 35 mesh (0.5 mm) gave consistent results. Materials finer than this could probably have been original constituents of the clay or have been reduced in size when the clay was pulverized. The material coarser than 35 mesh ranged from 5.8% to 11.2%. It can, therefore, be concluded that these sherds thought to be representative of the sand and shell-tempered pottery contained from 9% to 18% shell and 6%

to 11% sand that was 0.5mm or larger in diameter. These figures can, of course, be but rough indications of the range of shell and sand inclusions. There were many subrounded quartz grains in the sherds as well, as more angular sandstone and other rock fragments. Therefore, it is possible that sand was intentionally added to the clay as a tempering ingredient, but since sandy clay deposits are readily available at the Fort Ancient village site, it would be unwise to speak of intentional sand tempering until a great deal of on-the-site clay sampling had been done. Possibly, the cultural significance of the results obtained would not merit the effort involved.

A more accurate method of determining the amount of shell present in the sherds was used in the chemical laboratory of the archaeological Works Project Administration project sponsored by the University of Michigan. This efficient operation, of which the analytical activities were but a small part, was located in a school house in Detroit. Robert H. McDowell was the director of the project, and George I. Quimby served as acting director during the summer of 1938.

Five Fort Ancient fragments were included among a large series of calcium carbonate content determinations on pottery and plasters from several parts of the world carried out in the chemical laboratory of the WPA project under the direction of Mr. T. Giszczak. Powdered one gram samples from the pieces to be tested were dried, treated with dilute HCR, washed and filtered. The iron was removed from the filtrate with ferric hydroxide after which, following standard analytical procedures, the calcium was precipitated as calcium oxalate. This was then dissolved in sulfuric acid and titrated against a standard potassium permanganate solution. Two samples from each sherd were analyzed. If reasonable check results were not obtained, additional samples were measured.

The analyses showed that the five Fort Ancient sherds contained 9.4, 22.1, 24.2, 27.3, 27.6 and 41.1% shell. An examination of the sherds without reference to these results produced the same ordering of the series, but the three pieces in the 20% range were incorrectly ranked with respect to each other. There is a tendency to underestimate the amount of shell present by about 10% in this series, when the estimates are based on comparisons with the standard series of briquettes. The sherd with but 9.4% shell contained much sand.

The size of the shell flakes and the thickness of the laminae will, of course, influence one's estimate of the amount of shell material present. In some of the sherds, flakes up to 9 mm in length were observed, but this was most unusual. The largest individual flake seen was 7 x 4 mm in size. It is not difficult to crush calcined shell, so the size of the materials can be controlled.

This series of tests indicates that from one-fifth to two-fifths of the paste of shell-tempered pottery consists of shell particles. One-quarter to one-third of the batch as shell might account for much of the paste preparation of the potters at Fort Ancient. It must be remembered that when a potter crushes calcined shell, fine powder is also produced that is included in the batch. This can serve as a natural cementation ingredient, strengthening the body. I suggested in a paper presented at the SAA meetings in Boulder, Colorado, in 1963 that the success in the production of thin-walled and very low-fired shell-tempered pottery could be due, in part, to the development of cements when the powdered shell, clay and water were mixed together. These are the basic ingredients used in the preparation of some modern cements. Such a hardening agent, plus the support given to the body walls by the lamellar structure of the shell fragments and the reduction of shrinkage, makes possible the production of durable pottery with many different kinds of clay, even sandy ones. Hearth materials—ash together with calcined shells, detritus resulting from food preparation—would have been ingredients readily available to the potter who wished to make a wet batch of clay less sticky. The inclusion of ash will be considered at another time.

Degree of Firing

The examination of the surface and core color of sherds from the rim, body and basal areas of vessels, if carried out on a large number of sherds from a site from large and small vessels, together with thick and thin-walled ware, can produce a body of information that will help one understand the firing process at the site and may suggest more than one technique. If this examination is carried out with a knowledge of the pottery manufacturing processes known to have been used by the American Indians, much can be learned. Fewkes has admirably summarized much of this information. His useful and extensive bibliography includes articles by Harrington, Griffin, Griffin and Angell, and Holmes that are pertinent to a better understanding of the work of the pottery at Fort Ancient.

The sherds examined show that much of the shell-tempered ware has slightly oxidized surfaces with a dary gray core. Many pieces, however, have darkened surfaces beneath which one can find an oxidized zone when an edge is freshly fractured or ground smooth. The sandy ware has a very different color range, and the clay itself fires toward a red color. Often, the lip area of the rims show important color differences. Since the sherd sampling is too small to be statistically significant, no effort will be made here to analyze the color variations of the Fort Ancient Anderson Focus pottery in detail. It is notable, however, that the shell-tempered pottery tends to be darker than the more sandy ware. One wonders about variations in the firing techniques with time periods from Adena to Fort Ancient, the smothering of the hearth in the final stages of the firing, or the intentional smoking of the ware. Such studies would best be carried out at some major site (in terms of sherd generation with time horizons) at a current excavation.

The refiring of chips broken from sherds and the test firing of clays from the site, both under carefully controlled time, temperature and atmospheric conditions, can also produce useful results. Such firings of Anderson Focus sherds showed that most of the ware need not have been fired above 500° C., although from the standpoint of the complete elimination of the chemically-combined water in the clay, 600° C. would have been better.

Three sherds from Fort Ancient, Baum and Feurt were broken into fragments, and portions were refired at 500° and 600° for different periods of time. After five minutes at 500° C., the surfaces were freed of their soot, but there was no change in the dark color of the cores. After ten minutes, however, the cores were a much lighter gray in color. After forty minutes, the core was still more gray than the surfaces. At 600° C., there was a lightening of the core color after ten minutes, and a marked improvement occurred after twenty minutes; the core approaching the oxidized condition of the surfaces. Similar studies of the pottery from the Younge Site in Michigan were reported by Matson in 1939. Chips broken from several Fort Ancient sherds were fired to 800° to develop an optimum color, and were then cemented onto the parent sherds so that there would be a record of possible clay differences. In other studies, the clays from the site were washed to remove the coarser particles, and the finer-textured clay was then fired under test conditions with somewhat different oxidation rates in the less porous paste of the washed material. Studies of the porosity of Fort Ancient pottery were reported by Matson in 1941. He found that the shell temperated ware was a little more porous than that tempered with rock or sand.

In reviewing the data accumulated in the study of sherds from Fort Ancient and three clay samples obtained at the site, re-examining some of the sherds and petrographic thin sections, and conducting further tests of the clays, I find that I have much more of an interest in determining what can be learned from sherd studies at the site itself, before the materials are dispersed or stored, than in detailed laboratory analyses for this particular kind of pottery. Synthetic studies of shell tempering, some of which have been reported upon and others which are underway, as well as field experiments in the firing of such pottery, are useful. The potter at Fort Ancient had several textural variations in the clay resources available to her. She used a good quality clay when tempering it with shell, and she could produce good thin-walled vessels in part because of the chemical nature of the powdered shell. The uses to which such vessels were put and their frequency of distribution at a site are problems of continuing interest.

References Cited

Brownocker, J.A. "History of the Little Miami River." in *The Preglacial Drainage of Ohio, Ohio State Academy of Science*, Special Papers No. 3, 1900.

Dunnell, R.C., Hanson, Lee H., Jr., and Hardesty, Donald L. *Southeastern Archaeological Conference*. Bulletin No. 14, 1971.

———— . "The Prehistory of Fishtrap, Kentucky." *Yale University Publications in Anthropology*, No. 75, 1972.

Fewkes, Vladimir J. "Catawba Pottery-making, with Notes on Pamunkey Pottery-making, Cherokee Pottery-making, and Coiling." *Proceedings of the American Philosophical Society*, 88, No. 2:69–124, 1944.

Flynn, B.H. and M.S. "The Natural Features and Economic Development of the Sandusky, Maumee, Muskingum, and Miami Drainage Areas in Ohio. *U.S. Geological Survey*, Water Supply Paper 91, 1904.

Griffin, James B. and Angell, Carleton W. "An Experimental Study of the Technique of Indian Pottery Making." *Papers of the Michigan Academy of Science, Arts and Letters XX 1934*: 1–6 + 2 P1, 1934.

———— . "An Analysis of the Fort Ancient Culture." Notes from the Ceramic Repository for the Eastern United States, University of Michigan, March 1935: 10 pages, 1935.

———— . *The Fort Ancient Aspect, its Cultural and Chronological Position in Mississippi Valley Archaeology*. University of Michigan Press, Ann Arbor, 1943.

Guthe, Carl E. *Pueblo Pottery Making, a Study at the Village of San Ildefonso*. Papers of the Phillips Academy Southwestern Expedition, No. 2, New Haven, 1925.

———— . The Ceramic Repository for the Eastern United States, at the University of Michigan, under the auspices of the National Research Council. (Mimeographed, 6 pp.), 1927.

———— . "A Method of Ceramic Description." *Papers of the Michigan Academy of Science, Arts and Letters VIII*. 1927:23– 29, 1927.

Hanson, Lee H., Jr. *The Hardin Village Site*. University of Kentucky Press, 1966.

Leverett, Frank S. "Glacial Formations and Drainage Features of the Erie and Ohio Basins." *U.S. Geological Survey*, Monograph 41, 1902.

March, Benjamin. "Standards of Pottery Description." *Occasional Contributions from the Museum of Anthropology of the University of Michigan No. 3*. (Reprinted, 1967), 1934.

Matson, Frederick R. "Further Technological Notes on the Pottery of the Younge Site, Lapeer County, Michigan." *Papers of the Michigan Academy of Science, Arts and Letters*, XXIV, Pt. 4:11–23, 1939.

———— . "Porosity Studies of Ancient Pottery." *Ibid*, XXVI: 469–477, 1941.

Moorehead, Warren K. *Fort Ancient, Ohio*. Cincinnati, 1890.

Prufer, Olaf H. and Shane, Orrin C. III. *Blain Village and the Fort Ancient Tradition in Ohio.* The Kent State University Press, 1970.

Rafferty, Janet Elizabeth. The Development of the Ft. Ancient Tradition in Northern Kentucky. Ph.D. Dissertation. University of Washington, Seattle, 1974.

Shepard, Anna O. and Horton, Donald. "Conference on Archaeological Technology in Ceramics." *American Antiquity.* IV (4):358–359, 1939.

Table 3.1
Physical Properties of the Shell Tempered Clay Standards

Shell (Weight Percent)	Percentage Water of Plasticity	Percentage Linear Drying Shrinkage
0	26.0	8.1
5	28.0	7.0
10	22.4	5.0
20	23.3	4.3
30	21.5	3.6
40	19.2	1.9
50	17.8	2.6
60	13.8	0.0

Table 3.2
Estimated Shell Content of Sherds Compared with Standards

Percentage Shell	Number of Sherds	Percentage
5	4	2.3
10	22	12.7
10–20	16	9.2
20	87	50.2
20–30	31	17.9
30	14	8.1
40	1	0.6
	173	101.0

4

Functional Factors of Mica and Ceramic Burnishing

Dwight Wallace

Department of Anthropology,
State University of New York–Albany

Burnishing or polishing is a common feature in descriptions and analyses of preindustrial ceramic technology in the New World, where it represents the most common technique for producing "better" surface finishes. The more common term for this process among archaeologists is "polishing," but this term is used in the literature in materials science to refer to a fine abrasion or grinding of a surface. Therefore, "burnishing" will be used in this report for the process in question, the compaction through rubbing pressure of at least one of the body surfaces so that clay particles on the surface are aligned to the plane of the surface and reflected light, previously diffused, becomes concentrated or specular reflection, perceived as luster.

These discussions in anthropological literature have usually implied that burnishing was mainly for esthetic purposes (Shepard 1956, p. 124), although its effect on permeability has sometimes also been noted. The process has commonly been assumed to connote a higher level of ceramic technology, and Feinman (1980) considered burnishing as a factor in assessing the comparative economics of ceramic manufacture. The literature of materials science has not, to my knowledge, dealt with

Revised version of paper presented at the symposium "New Approaches to Ceramic Technology," American Anthropological Association, Annual Meetings, 1982. Not for quotation without permission of author. Acknowledgments: We wish to thank Dr. William Lanford of Physics and Dr. Karlene Davis of Geology, both at SUNY-Albany, and Dr. Robert Doremus and Brian Tracy of the Materials Science Division of Rensselaer Polytechnic Institute for their invaluable help and advice. Any mistakes are our own.

the burnishing of greenware bodies, undoubtedly because the technique dropped out of use by potters in the tradition of Western Civilization more than a millenia ago.

An analysis of ceramics from the protohistoric site of Utatlan, near Santa Cruz del Quiche, center of the Quiche Maya of highland Guatemala, indicated that burnished wares occurred in such high frequencies—80% at the lowest in any excavational units—that they obviously represented vessels of domestic function as well as ones for more specialized purposes. It would be significant if this time-consuming process of burnishing were utilized so widely simply to satisfy a desire for more attractive pottery, whether the attraction were motivated by esthetics, a desire for excellence, or expectations of the potter's clientele. In surveying the literature on ceramics in materials science, a graduate student, Carlos Viana, noted a book with an intriguing title, *Strengthening of Ceramics* (1979, pp. 12f, 31). The author, Henry P. Kirchner, notes that the strengthening effect of glazing has been known for centuries and strengthening by rapid cooling noted some 30 years ago; his own work shows that both glazing and quenching in silicone oil on removal from the kiln increases strength by up to 50% for high strength bodies he was testing. The increased strength derives from the surfaces being under compressed tension, having shrunk somewhat less than the more bulky interiors. The compressed state is not inherent to glazes, but the result of the known effect of using a particular glaze on a particular body; for the case of quenching, it is the result of that process itself.

The simple mechanical explanation for the increased strength derived from the compressed surfaces is that sufficient distortion must occur simply to release the surface from this compressed state before it passes through a state of equilibrium into a state of tensile stress, at some point during which crack initiation will occur and the ceramic will subsequently fail in a brittle manner. This failure threshold will be reached either sooner or at a lower force if the surface is not in a compressed state. This surface compression as a static state should not be confused with fracture-causing stresses, which may also be compressive.

From Kirchner's work we predicted that burnishing would strengthen a ceramic body. Although the compaction created by the burnishing does not in itself create the compressed state, it seemed likely the compacted surface would shrink less than the core during firing, leaving the surface under compression. The mechanics of arriving at the compressed state are, therefore, different from either quenching or glazing, but both of the latter also derive from different processes. Because of a problem in quantifying luster, to be noted later, the hypothesis is best stated simply that ceramics with burnished surfaces will be stronger than unburnished ones that are otherwise the same, if the burnished side is placed in tensile stress by flexural or impact forces.

An obvious approach would be to test characteristics of the actual sherds. What would then be needed would be a way to differentiate between strength derived from the curvature of the sherd from that of the material itself. Thickness of the sherds, degree of burnish, finish on the other surface from the burnished one, and the exact ingredients of the sherd body would all have to be controlled in any experiment using the sherds themselves, or even experiments using clays from the Quiche Basin.

However, an additional possibility was to conduct more strictly experimental tests; that is, tests which were on ceramic specimens prepared in a manner so that the variables involved could be controlled, requiring use of materials not identical to that of the sherds. This type of approach has been used with increasing frequency; the work of Rye (1981) can be used as a good example. A full understanding of any ceramic variable cannot be obtained from such controlled but artificial experiments, but neither can tests using only the sherds or examples made from identical materials. Such knowledge comes from a comparison of as many tests of different combinations of variables as possible.

The Tests

Vessel strength derives from a combination of the strength of the ceramic material and the strength derived from vessel form. Only material strength will be considered here, since the comparative strength of different vessel forms is not the question. Secondly, the strength test will be applied to a particular shape of test tile, but the test results are converted to pounds per square inch needed to fracture the example, the result applicable to any shape or thickness of the same ceramic body. Lastly, there are various types of strengths of ceramics, all but tensile strength being closely related. Impact strength is pertinent to the initial circumstance causing vessel breakage, but secondary fracturing caused by an impact is, in fact, due largely to flexural or bending stresses. Also, impact fracture force varies with the angle of force application and the shape and material of the object or item impacting the ceramic item; sherd curvature would also introduce an additional type of strengthening during testing. As a result, it would be difficult to equate the test situation with the variety of situations under which breakage of vessels occurs. Therefore, the advantages of exact replication is largely lost, and flexural strength tests are considered sufficient to represent the major type of force involved.

Cylindrical rods averaging 6.5 mm in diameter were prepared for the test; this shape is the preferred one for tests of flexural strength, being free of effects deriving from such surface features as the number of angular changes in the profile when the material is put under a flexing load (Doremus 1982, p. 171). Commerical clay was used in order to ensure consistency between the test cases. A terracotta clay was used because it gives a ware closer in porosity to that produced by preindustrial potters and also because it contained a grog temper of uniform quantity and grain size, again closer to the inclusions that commonly occur in preindustrial wares. A buff-firing clay was also used to include an untempered clay and also a different clay mineral type. Half of the cylinders were burnished with a wetted glass rod in the leather hard state; all were fired together at 800° C. in an electric kiln.

As recommended by Bronitsky (1981, p. 8), testing was done on an Instron apparatus using a four-point jig. The load applied was recorded mechanically on graph paper. All test sets had more than 30 cases. The test results (Table 4.1) showed relatively low variability within all sets. The terracotta burnished set averaged 28% stronger than the unburnished terracotta, the buff-firing burnished set averaged 17.3% stronger than the unburnished buff-firing examples. All differences were significant at well below the .05 level.

Since the cylinders were burnished on both sides, they are the equivalent of a vessel wall burnished on both sides. The results of this test are not directly applicable to cases of burnishing on one surface only, since the two surfaces are under different stresses when either an impact or flexing force is applied, one side under compression, the other under tension. Therefore, tests were conducted with buff-firing clay examples burnished on one-half circumference side only; half were tested with the burnished surface opposite in orientation from the other half, the results are also shown in Table 4.1. With the burnished surface on the side under tensile stress, the strength gain over the unburnished examples was exactly the same as when the entire surfaces were burnished, while the gain was only 9.1% when the burnished surfaces were on the side of compressive stress. These results are somewhat more striking than expected; although burnish on the compressive stress side does give some strength, burnish on all sides gives no greater strength than burnish on the side of tensile stress only. These tests of one-side burnishing should be repeated with flat-sided specimens before the exact effect will be clear. However, there is no doubt that the secondary flexural fracturing resulting from an initial impact fracture will be lessened when the impact is on the surface which is burnished.

To translate these results to ceramic vessels, we can assume that most breakage is caused by impact forces to the exterior of the vessel. A vessel burnished on the interior or on both interior and exterior would definitely be stronger than the same vessel without burnishing. However, a vessel burnished only on the exterior can be expected to gain some strength over an unburnished one.

It is important to note that the comparisons must be made between vessels of the same shape and thickness, since both are alternative variables in giving strength to a vessel. Also, if different clays, different firing temperatures, different body preparation, or different amounts and types of inclusions are used, then the amounts of strengthening due to burnishing will not be directly comparable. But there is excellent reason to assume that all compaction of surfaces of any type of clay will produce some degree of compressive stress and, therefore, some degree of strengthening.

As noted earlier, it would be ideal to correlate degree of burnishing with degree of strengthening. Compaction itself could be measured, but with difficulty; the degree of luster is a more easily obtained measure and can be expected to correlate with degree of compaction if used on comparable clay bodies. However, there is good reason to assume that the degree of luster would not correlate exactly with the degree of compaction when comparing two different clay bodies, since clays vary widely in the ease with which they attain luster through burnishing (Shepard 1956, p. 123).

The physics of luster are unfortunately complex, and the quantification of luster by the most direct measure, the amount of reflected light, is affected by the degree and nature of the curvature of the lustrous surface; in materials science, such measurements are done on flat test tiles using a reflectometer. In addition, burnishing itself causes a change in value and chroma of the clay color. Finally, reflectivity varies between colors, making simple comparisons of readings impossible; a white surface will give a much higher reading than a black surface of equal luster. Even highlights are affected by color differences. Tests on the reliability of reflectometer readings and methods of adjusting for color differences are in the process of being carried out in our laboratory (Crane n.d.)

While the tests showed that burnishing increases the strength of a ware, appreciably so if on the surface opposite to that most likely to receive an impact fracturing force, it is worth noting that interpretations of the intent of the original potters is not so simple; whether a given case had been done with the intent of strengthening or of esthetic enhancement would require additional data. The case of a thin, burnished fine ware would be an illustrative case, since the thinness may have been encouraged by the strengthening effect of the burnishing. For Utatlan ceramics, the use of burnishing on a wide range of pottery of domestic use, devoid of other decoration, does fit the same argument.

The questionable added strength for jars polished only on the outside is partially explained by the difficulty of burnishing the interior; but the jar form also is a reminder that decreased permeability may also be a reason for burnishing.

The strengthening effect of burnishing could possibly have been predicted, since the surface condition of any material is critical in the initiation of fractures from that surface, and burnishing cannot be accomplished unless the surface is free of irregularities. If this line of reasoning is followed, it is possible that slipping will also result in some degree of strengthening, since it results in a more consistent surface and may also possibly leave compressed surfaces when fired. This and various other features of burnishing should be further tested.

Shepard (1963, p. 125) noted a case in which the potters claimed to have to sacrifice strength to obtain the burnished luster desired. There is no evidence that burnished wares were fired at lower temperatures by Mesoamerican or Andean potters—if anything, just the opposite. Shepard's potters were apparently producing a special decorative burnished black ware or were using a clay that burnishes particularly well but shrinks a great deal during firing, giving the fine, superficial buckling cracks that can occur either with burnished surfaces or a glaze that does not fit the body to which it is applied. Neither the burnished test rods nor the many burnished pieces using local garden clay produced over the years by our students showed any loss of luster when fired well into the range used by precolumbian potters. The association of burnishing with finer, thinner wares may also have obscured the practical value of burnishing.

References Cited

Bronitsky, Gordon. *Materials Science Approaches in Archeology: A Southwestern Example.* (ms. in possession of author). n.d.

Crane, Donald. *Quantifying Burnished Luster.* (ms. in possession of author). n.d.

Doremus, Robert H. "Fracture and Fatigue of Glass." *Treatise on Materials Science and Technology.* Vol. 22, pp. 169–239. Academic Press, New York, 1982.

Kirchner, Henry P. *Strengthening of Ceramics.* Marcel Dekker, Inc., New York, 1979.

Loughnan, F.C. *Chemical Weathering of the Silicate Minerals.* American Elsevier Publishing Co., Inc., New York, 1969.

Rye, Owen. *Pottery Technolgoy: Principles and Reconstruction.* Taraxacum, Washington, D.C., 1981.

Shepard, Anna O. *Ceramics for the Archaeologist.* Carnegie Institution of Washington, Washington, D.C., 1954.

Warren, A.H. "The Micaceous Pottery of the Rio Grande." *Archaeological Society of New Mexico, Anthropological Papers.* No. 6, pp. 149–165, 1981.

Table 4.1
Flexural Strength Test Results

Clay Preparation Types*	N	Ave. PSI	Stan. Dev.	Stan. Error
Tests of Burnish				
Terracotta				
Green, unburn.	46	122.0	22.64	3.20
Unburnished	46	227.9	24.76	3.65
Burnished	33	291.5	30.79	5.36
Buff-firing				
Unburnished	30	355.6	56.15	10.25
Burn., 1 side, on compression	30	404.3	39.72	7.25
Burn., 1 side, on tension	20	432.8	23.01	5.15
Burnished all over	30	432.9	58.72	10.14
Tests of Mica Temper				
Refractory clay				
Green, plain	21	116.9	22.59	4.93
Green, mica	15	110.4	23.20	5.99
Plain	29	198.9	32.10	5.96
Mica temper, 1:10	40	212.7	37.88	5.99
Mica temper, 1:5	19	236.0	30.43	6.98

*All non-green examples fired at 800°C.

5

Some Techniques Used by the Potters of Tell Hadidi During the Second Millennium B.C.

Abraham van As

Institute of Pottery Technology,
Leiden University, Leiden, The Netherlands

Introduction

This article presents a technological study of pottery from the second millennium B.C. which was found at the Syrian site of Tell Hadidi. This is one of three archeological sites[1] which between 1972 and 1975 were excavated under direction of Professor H. J. Franken and where collections of pottery were assembled for technological research. The objective of this study is the application of certain ideas which H. J. Franken and J. Kalsbeek have developed during their study of ceramic material from Tell Deir Alla in Jordan (Franken 1969).

The research was made possible thanks to the financial support from The Netherlands Organization for the Advancement of Pure Research. It took place within the context of the rescue excavations which were carried out during the 1970's in the Tabqa area (the present day Lake Assad), in northwestern Syria (Fig. 5.1) under the overall supervision of the Department of Antiquities of the Syrian Arabic Republic, in close cooperation with UNESCO.

Tell Hadidi and the Dating of the Pottery

Tell Hadidi was located, before the creation of Lake Assad, along the right bank of the Euphrates River, in northwestern Syria (Fig. 5.1). The tell, which may perhaps be identified with the city of Azu (Dornemann 1980:219), consists of an elevated part, the so-called High Tell (250 $\times$

400 m), and a lower section, or "Low Tell," which extends over a distance of approximately 500 m eastward along the Euphrates.

The earliest occupation of the site started around 2300 B.C., in the Early Bronze Age (ca. 3200–2000 B.C.). The prosperity of the area went into a decline after the Hittite conquest. Finds from the Roman and Islamic period indicate that the tell was also inhabited in later times. For more detailed information about the tell and its history I refer the reader to various studies by Dornemann (1978; 1979; 1980; 1982, etc.).

The pottery which will be discussed in this article derives from excavation areas A/AA and M, both located on the High Tell (Fig. 5.2). The ceramics from area A/AA were found among the rubble of a house. The same point applies to the pottery from area M (for a plan, see Dornemann 1980: Fig. 5.10). It can be stated on the basis of the unusual architecture and uncommon items which were found in the same context, such as a stone mask that the ceramics from Hadidi M do not derive from a normal house. The building materials and the construction of the building are very similar to a structure from a somewhat earlier period which was excavated to the south of the house (see Dornemann 1980: Fig. 5.10). Inside this earlier building, which was excavated by Dornemann and his team[2], they found cylinder seals, sealings and clay tablets which have been dated to the 15th century B.C. (Dornemann 1978:23; idem 1980:222, 223). These finds provide a *terminus post quem* for the adjoining structure where the pertinent pottery was found. Comparisons of the pottery from the building which was excavated in area M with ceramics from other archaeological sites indicate that the material should be dated to the Late Bronze Age I (ca. 1550–1400 B.C.) (cf. Dornemann 1979; 1981).

In order to obtain an acceptable date for the pottery from area A/AA we are left with certain parallels in shape. These comparisons date to a time during the Middle Bronze Age (ca. 2000–1550 B.C.) (Dornemann 1979; idem 1981; idem in press). The precise dividing line between the Middle and Late Bronze Age cannot always clearly be indicated (Matthers 1981). There seems to be a high degree of continuity in ceramic shapes. It is for this reason that the pottery from area A/AA is discussed together with the pottery from area M.

Basic Idea and Approach

The approach to the Tell Hadidi pottery from the second millennium B.C. which was found in areas A/AA and M, is based on the idea that a typological study of excavated pottery should be based on an analysis of the manufacturing techniques of that ceramic material (Franken 1969; idem 1975:26-35). There is no deviation from a typology based on an analysis of the shapes. In a technological typology, however, an attempt is made not merely to describe and analyze, but also to explain the shape of a specific pot. When setting up such a technological typology, the whole process of production needs to be involved: the clay used by the potters; the question how the clay was prepared; how the pots were shaped; what kind of tools were used in the process, and how the pots were dried and fired. There are no independent sources to be consulted as regards the function of the pots.

There are no written data about the pottery which is described in the present study, which may be used to describe the manner in which these ceramics were manufactured. The answer only lies in a study of the pottery itself.

A piece of ceramic forms a complex artifact. All its aspects, such as the basic material; its shape; the color; the firing technique, etc., are all interrelated. The same point goes for the different manufacturing stages. An analysis of the form technique is carried out with the help of a careful study of the pottery. On the basis of possible traces of various manufacture stages, it is often possible to reconstruct the complete manufacturing process.

Most of the reconstructions which are based on a careful analysis of the pottery, can subsequently be verified by experiments. Such experiments should show the same traces of manufacture on the same type of pottery. When such an experiment proves successful, it may be accepted that the reconstruction is reliable.

Knowledge of the applied basic material is very important for a technological study of pottery. For various reasons (see Franken 1983; van As 1984[1]; idem 1984[2]) in this study preference has been given to simple and low-cost material analyses. On the basis of the results of these material analyses it is possible to see whether further physical-chemical laboratory research is needed in order to solve specific problems. For the simple analyses, fresh breaks in the pottery and thin sections were studied under the microscope, in order to study the non-plastic material both quantitatively and qualitatively. By firing the test sherds in an oxidizing atmosphere, the fortuitous colors of the sherds could be eliminated which made it possible to set up a classification on the basis of the firing color. In addition, the firing tests gave an impression of the original firing temperature and atmosphere (reducing/neutral/oxidizing).

The Form Techniques

Complete Shapes and Large Fragments

1. *Pottery thrown from the cone (Fig. 5.3).* Most of the pots which had been thrown from the cone had been moved in a clockwise direction.

Only two (Fig. 5.3: 6, 7) of the seven vessels had been thrown in an anti-clockwise direction. Sometimes the shoulder and neck were finished with a potter's rib (Fig. 5.3: 4, 5). In all cases, after scraping, the surface of the vessel was smoothed with wet hands or with a sponge. In some cases the body of the vessel was scraped while being turned (Fig. 5.3: 4, 5, 6, 7). In one example the base was scraped to a ring base (Fig 5.3: 2). Also a handle was attached. The remaining vessels had flatly scraped bases.

2. *Pottery thrown from one piece of clay (Fig. 5.4)*. In eight examples the direction of the turn could not be determined. In the remaining twenty cases, however, the pot was thrown anti-clockwise in seventeen cases, and clockwise in the remaining three cases. Where the vessel was subsequently not scraped, there are sometimes traces of the use of a rib. These are traces of wet scraping, which can sometimes be found on the interior wall of the pot (Fig. 5.4: 1, 8, 10, 11), or on the exterior at the shoulder (Fig. 5.4: 10, 11). At the end of the manufacturing process, the surface is often smoothed with a wet hand or sponge. This can be seen on the interior (Fig. 5.4: 4, 15) and on the exterior (Fig. 5.4: 7, 24, 25, 26, 27). When the vessels were thrown from one piece of clay, a considerable amount of scraping was needed in order to achieve the correct thickness of the wall and base. When the vessel was leather hard, it was put upside down on the potter's wheel, attached with a piece of clay, and subsequently the pot was scraped to the desired thickness while turning. The bottom part of the body of the vessel, often as far as the largest diameter of the pot, and the base were thus scraped to the correct shape and thickness. The base could be round (Fig. 5.4: 30); flat (Fig. 5.4: 1, 2, 3, 4, 5, 6, 7, 8, 16); pointed (Fig. 5.4: 20), or with a ring base (Fig. 5.4: 10, 11, 12, 14, 15, 17, 19, 22, 24, 25, 26, 27). The scraping also played a role in the decoration of the vessel. In a number of cases scraping resulted in a ridge on the shoulder (Fig. 5.4: 10, 11, 12, 14, 17). Other decoration techniques which were encountered when studying the vessels which had been thrown from one piece of clay included: applied bands with incisions, attached to the shoulder (Fig. 5.4: 24, 25, 26, 27), and polishing (Fig. 5.4: 10, 19, 20, 22). Sometimes only the shoulder was polished (Fig. 5.4: 15), while in others it was but the shoulder and body (Fig. 5.4: 10, 22). Only one vessel was completely polished (Fig. 5.4: 12).

3. *Pottery which was thrown on a sand-covered support plate on the potter's wheel (Fig. 5.5)*. The exterior was sponged. This technique has only been met once among the ceramic repertoire of Tell Hadidi.

4. *Pottery thrown on a slow wheel, and built up in coils (Fig. 5.6)*. From the 55 examples, only seven were turned in an anti-clockwise direction, while eleven vessels were thrown clockwise. In 37 cases the direction

could not be determined. The vessels were slowly thrown in coils. For illustrations of this production manner, see Combes and Louis (1967: Pl. IV 2 c) and van As and Jacobs (1985: Fig. 6). A rope was often used on the outside to support the vessel and to prevent its collapse. Impressions of this rope, when not removed with scraping, are sometimes still visible (Fig. 5.6: 12, 13, 15, 21, 22, 25, 26, 49, 51, 52, 53). During the slow throwing process, use was often made of the rib. This can be detected by the wet scraping traces. These traces can be seen on the interior and exterior, at various places of the vessel, namely: all the interior of the vessel (Fig. 5.6: 6, 18, 22, 23, 24, 44, 46, 48, 49, 50, 52, 53); on the interior as far as the greatest diameter (Fig. 5.6: 21, 25, 26); on the interior, above the greatest diameter (Fig. 5.6:45), and on the exterior above the greatest diameter (Fig. 5.6: 10, 17, 20, 26, 29, 31, 32, 41, 43, 50, 51, 52). There are also traces of scraping which were made when the clay was less wet, but certainly not yet leather hard. These traces are visible on the inside (Fig. 5.6: 1, 12, 16, 19, 30, 33, 34, 35, 40, 47, 54); on the inside of the base as high as the shoulder or halfway the shoulder (Fig. 5.6: 28, 39); on the inside above the greatest diameter (Fig. 5.6: 29, 31, 36); on the outside as high as the shoulder (Fig. 5.6: 39) and on the neck (Fig. 5.6: 37). Two vessels, when almost leather hard, had been scraped on the inside as far as the greatest diameter (Fig. 5.6: 32, 45). The wall was put upside down on the wheel and then the exterior was scraped while turning, either completely (Fig. 5.6: 6, 7, 8, 9, 16, 18, 19, 21, 24, 25, 27, 28, 30, 34, 40, 44, 45, 46, 57, 49, 51, 54), either from the base upwards towards the largest diameter (Fig. 5.6: 11, 12, 13, 15, 17, 20, 22, 23, 29, 32, 26, 41, 50). The base was also scraped into various shapes, namely: flat (Fig. 5.6: 2, 3, 4, 8, 9, 25, 33, 35); ring base (Fig. 5.6: 6, 7, 26, 27); round (Fig. 5.6: 14, 20, 32, 34, 46, 47, 54), and slightly convex-shaped (Fig. 5.6: 11, 12, 13, 15, 21, 22, 23, 24, 25, 28, 49, 51, 52, 53). In the latter bases, and in those which were round in shape, there was sometimes a hole with a diameter of ca. 1.3 cm (Fig. 5.6: 12, 13, 20, 21, 23, 24, 51, 53). The large vessels with perforated bases were used for the storage of grain (Dornemann 1981: 41). The vessels with a rounded slightly convex-shaped base were dried while standing in the sand; this can be shown by the sand that is stuck to the clay (Fig. 5.6: 49, 51, 52, 54). In some cases a ring base was not scraped out, but separately affixed (Fig. 5.6: 16, 17, 18, 45, 46). In one example the pot was not scraped after it was put upside down on the wheel, but while held in the potter's hands (Fig. 5.6: 5). Except for polishing, this group of vessels is decorated in a similar manner as the previous group: incised line decoration (Fig. 5.6: 17, 18, 25); comb decoration (Fig. 5.6: 10, 20, 22, 23, 25, 38, 39, 49, 51, 52, 53); ridges (Fig. 5.6: 11, 23, 26) and applied bands (Fig. 5.6: 13, 15), sometimes in

combination with comb decoration (Fig. 5.6: 51, 53). In two cases the
rim is provided with grooves (Fig. 5.6: 38, 44). The rims are thickened,
or not (Fig. 5.6: 1, 27, 42). The thickening was done in various manners
(see below). One of these manners was the folding double of the rim
(Fig. 5.6: 2, 3, 14, 28). Sometimes the vessels, or parts of them, are
smoothed with wet hands or a wet sponge, after scraping (Fig. 5.6: 2,
4, 12, 15, 32, 36, 46, 47). When handles are present, these are rolled
(Fig. 5.6: 43), or after rolling somewhat pulled (Fig. 5.6: 17, 18, 29, 30,
32, 33, 34, 35, 36). In the latter case the handle is strengthened with
a piece of clay, at the place where it is attached to the shoulder of the
pot.

5. *Thrown and thrown closed pottery (Fig. 5.7).* Only three examples
were found. One of these was thrown in a clockwise direction (Fig. 5.7:
1); a second was thrown in the opposite direction (Fig. 5.7: 3). The
direction of throwing of the third vessel could not be determined. The
neck was attached on an opening made in the body where the thrown
part passes into the thrown closed part.[3] The interior of Fig. 5.7: 2 was
"scraped" while still wet. The upright thrown part of the pot illustrated
in Fig. 5.7: 2 was scraped on the exterior. The neck was scraped in all
three cases. The handles were rolled and pulled (Fig. 5.7: 1, 2). One
of the vessels was completely polished (Fig. 5.7: 3).

6. *Handmade pottery (Fig. 5.8).* Among the pertinent repertoire there
is one dish which was made by hand without the application of a
potter's wheel. The dish was made in a mold. One clay coil was attached.
The outside was sponged.

The studied sample from Tell Hadidi A and M consisted of 96 almost
complete shapes. In Table 5.1 an indication is given of some reconstructed
manufacturing techniques which were used for the pertinent repertoire.

Whether the percentages in Table 5.1 of the various manufacturing
techniques are representative for the pottery which was used during the
Middle and Late Bronze Age at Tell Hadidi, depends on the representa-
tiveness of the excavated sample. The sample was determined by the
character and function of the rooms from the buildings in which the
pottery was found. Because manufacturing techniques and the function
of the pottery are closely related, some techniques may receive more
emphasis than warranted (see for example the slowly thrown storage
vessels, built up in coils, which were found in the storage rooms of the
building in Area M).

Sherds

Base sherds: The base sherds may indicate more clearly than other
types of sherds what type of manufacture has been used to produce

the vessel. All techniques which were recognized when studying the complete shapes could also be found when studying the base sherds.

Rim sherds: The rim sherds are not really diagnostic for the manufacturing technique of the pertinent vessel. On the basis of the rim sherds, however, the technical finishing off of the rim can be studied. By comparing the shapes of the rims with those of the complete pots from Tell Hadidi, it sometimes proved possible to establish the shape of the vessel to which the rim sherd belonged.

The rim sherds could be distinguished in thickened and unthickened rims. Reasons to thicken a rim may be as follows:

1. to strengthen the vessel for use.
2. to strengthen the joint between rim and handle.
3. to serve as a holding point.
4. to give the lid a firm position.
5. to correct a rim which had become oblique.

For the thickened rims the following technological differentiation could be made:

1. pressed up (Fig. 5.9: 1).
2. pressed up/pressed down (Fig. 5.9: 2).
3. pressed down (Fig. 5.9: 3).
4. folded (Fig. 5.9: 4).
5. folded/pressed down (Fig. 5.9: 5).

Firing Temperature and Kiln Atmosphere

When studying the original firing temperature and kiln atmosphere, account should be taken of the fact that the vessels from Hadidi M and some of the pots from Hadidi A/AA were fired again when the building in which these ceramics were found was burned down. It is for this reason that the original firing temperature cannot be determined. The temperature of the second firing may have been much higher than the kiln temperature at the time of the first, original firing. Also the kiln atmosphere may have been different. The firing atmosphere of the secondary fire was in certain places very reducing. This would explain the grey-black color of some sherds found in the ruins. The sherds which were found outside these areas do not have this grey-black color. After restoration, some of the vessels therefore offer a very varied spectacle with sherds of various colors. On the basis of the sherds which were found outside the reducing atmosphere of the secondary fire, the impression exists that the vessels were originally fired in a neutral or lightly reducing atmosphere.

The Applied Basic Materials

To exclude all variables which occur with fires, and thus to arrange the firing color of the clay which was used in antiquity, a number of test sherds were fired again, in an electric kiln in oxidizing atmosphere, to a temperature of respectively 750° C.; 1050° C.; and 1150° C. After firing to a temperature of 1050° C., the following three groups could be differentiated:

1. The test sherds of Fig. 5.3: 4, 7; 5.4: 8, 10, 11, 12, 15, 22, 29; 5.5; 5.6: 1, 5, 6, 20, 26, 29, 31, 38, 40, 41, 42, 43, 44, 45, 53, have a uniform color (10 YR-8/2, very pale brown). Interpretation: hardly or no presence of iron.

2. The nucleus of the test sherds of Figs. 5.3: 6; 5.4: 1, 28; 5.6: 21, 22, 25, 28, 34, 39, 48 is reddish yellow (5 YR-6/6). The surface of the sherd is white (10 YR-8/2). Interpretation: the clay contains little iron. There is no "scum" layer[4] on the surface.

3. The inside of the test sherds of Figs. 5.3: 2, 3, 5; 5.4: 17; 5.6: 11, 16, 17, 18, 19, 23, 24, 30, 32, 33, 35, 36, 37, 46, 49, 52, 54; 5.7: 1, 2, 3 have a red (10 R-4/6) or light red (10 R-6/6) surface. Sometimes this layer crumbles off easily. In some cases the red color had penetrated deeper into the body of the sherd. At a temperature of 1150° C. the red layer tends to sinter. This phenomenon cannot be explained as a slip layer. On sherds that were not fired again, nothing indicated such a layer. The phenomenon can perhaps be explained by the contents of the original pot which may have included much iron. The remains of this iron would be responsible for the red color of the test sherds which were fired again. Another possibility which has to be considered is that the original contents of the vessel contained acid. This would have leached out the lime in the vessel, as a result of which the iron contents on the inside would have become dominant. This could explain the red color. The occurrence of the red layer, however, could not be correlated to a particular shape of pot, so that the above hypothesis becomes unlikely. To test the hypotheses, a laboratory analysis was made of four sherds. This was done at the Department of Soil Science and Geology at the Agricultural University at Wageningen (Prof. Dr. L. van de Plas). Roentgen diffraction research showed that the red layer on three of the sherds contained some hematite. This hematite could not be detected in the fourth sherd.[5]

The third group may either belong to the first (without any iron present), or the second (iron containing). A more precise identification is difficult to make in the case where the red zone penetrated as far as the core. A comparison of the different firing color groups with the various shapes and manufacturing techniques does not indicate a relationship. The difference between the firing color groups 1 and 2 is not important. Both clays may have been found in close proximity, and they were apparently applied side by side for various techniques. The study of the non-plastic additions to the clay was made with the help of a 40× magnification. Quartz, feldspar, basalt and micro-fossils could be detected. In all studied cases the size of the quartz grains was less than 1 mm. Within this group it is difficult to make a classification. While still trying to do so, the following remarks can be made (see Fig. 5.10). The grain size from 21 of the 92 sherds ranged from 0.1 to 0.4 mm (A). For 64 of 92 investigated samples the size lay between 0.3 and 0.5 mm (C). For three sherds, the quartz grains varied from 0.2 to 0.5 mm (B). These three samples constitute the transition from group A to C. The remaining four samples constitute extremes (0.1: 0.2–0.6 mm and 0.2–1.0 mm). Within the main groups of A (0.1–0.4 mm) and B (0.2–0.5 mm) the following weight percentages[6] of the quartz could be determined: (1) 2% and less; (2) 3–8%; (3) 9% and more (see Table 5.2). In Table 5.2[7] there is also an indication of the amount of micro-fossils presented: a. none; b. few (less than 1%); c. 1–3%; d. 4–7%. As with the groups which were based on the firing color, no correlation could be established between the various groups indicated in this paragraph and certain shapes or manufacturing techniques. For instance, the bowls which are illustrated in Fig. 5.4: 10,11, and which, although different in secondary manufacturing techniques (Fig. 5.4: 10 is polished, contrary to Fig. 5.4: 11), are identical in primary manufacturing technique, belong to different material groups, C2a and A2a respectively. The jugs, Fig. 5.6: 33 and 35, belong to material groups A2c and C2a, while the jugs Fig. 5.6: 32 and 34, belong to group C2c. The small pots, thrown from the cone (Fig. 5.3: 3, 5), two large pots (Fig. 5.6: 17, 19) and a large storage jar (Fig. 5.6: 52), were all three thrown on a slow wheel (in coils), and all belong to the same material group, namely C2c. Fig. 11 shows the relationship between shape, manufacturing technique and the material of the above mentioned examples. A comparison of the material groups with the pottery shapes and manufacturing techniques shows that the material was apparently suitable for the manufacture of all existing shapes in the Bronze Age repertoire from Tell Hadidi. In other words, the tolerance of the material was considerable. This is not surprising, from the point of view of the potter. With the grain sizes and percentages of the quartz all the primary and secondary manufacturing techniques could be executed. There are no indications to suggest that the quartz was deliberately added. The size of quartz grains and their percentage in the clay varies with the place where it was found and with the season of deposition. The basic material could be applied without further preparations.

Conclusion

The technological study of the second millennium B.C. potter from Tell Hadidi resulted in a technological description of the craft aspects of this pottery. Such a study has not been carried out up till now and may be used as a starting point for future technological pottery research in Syria. This may serve to establish a firmer foundation for typological studies of pottery from this area.

Notes

1. The other sites are: Jebel Aruda (Uruk period); Ta'as (Islamic period).

2. An American team from Milwaukee has been working at Tell Hadidi from 1974 onward, under the direction of Dr. R.H. Dornemann (Milwaukee Public Museum).

3. For the "throwing closed" technique see Franken 1975: Fig. 12, 19, 20.

4. Scum is an insoluble layer on the surface of the pot. It is created during the firing process. It consists of salts and sulphur, derived from the clay and the kiln fumes respectively.

5. From each of the four samples (1–4) there are two sherds, indicated with a and b. All a samples have a clearly more noticeable yellow matrix than the b samples. The latter have a somewhat more red matrix. In addition, all a samples, but one, have a dark red surface on one side. With the help of a Guinier camera, two Röentgen diffraction photographs were made of both sides of each sherd. The result of this particular study can be summarized as follows: (1) All samples (16x) are identical as regards the main composite materials, and consist in the main of quartz, pyroxene and feldspar; (2) the feldspar line are in all samples so diffuse, that only with the help of a 4,03 Å-line it could be determined that here it concerns plagioclase; (3) the pyroxene lines are also not very clear: in two samples (1 and 4) they are so diffuse, that the augite/diopsite-triplet 2.99 Å-2.95 Å. 290 Å, which is clearly present in all other samples, could not be detected; (4) the dark red surface of three samples (1a, 3a and 4a) also contains a little hematite. In the other samples this could not be found; and (5) the weak lines, especially in two samples (1a and 2b), do not belong to one of the already mentioned minerals, and indicate the presence of a little, non-identified, other crystalline material.

6. The determination of the weight percentages of quartz was done by comparison with a reference collection with known weight percentages.

7. This list only includes test sherds of complete shapes and large fragments.

References Cited

As, A. van. "Reconstructing the Potter's Craft." in S.E. van der Leeuw and A.C. Pritchard (eds.), *The Many dimensions of Pottery.* Amsterdam: 131–164, 1984.

As, A. van. "Pottery Technology and Physicoscientific Analyses of Ceramics." *Newsletter II Department of Pottery Technology Leiden:* 10–13, 1984.

As, A. van and Jacobs, L. "Technological Research of Palaeo-and Meso-Babylonian Pottery from Tell ed-Deir (Iraq)—a report. *Newsletter III Department of Pottery Technology Leiden:* 15–26, 1985.

Combès, J.L. and Louis, A. *Les Potiers de Djerba,* Tunis, 1967.

Dornemann, R.H. "Tell Hadidi: a Bronze Age City on the Euphrates." *Archaeology.* 31 (6):20–26, 1978.

———. "Tell Hadidi: A Millennium of Bronze Age City Occupation." *Annual of the American Schools of Oriental Research.* 44:113–151, 1979.

———. "Tell Hadidi: an Important Center of the Mittannian Period and Earlier." in J.C.P. Margueron (ed.), *Le Moyen Euprate, zone de contacts et d'echanges, Actes due Colloque de Strasbourg.* 10–12 mars 1977:217–234, 1980.

———. "The Late Bronze Age Pottery Tradition at Tell Hadidi, Syria." *Bulletin of the American Schools of Oriental Research.* 241:29–47, 1981.

———. "Tell Hadidi." *Archiv Für Orientforschung.* 28:219–223, 1982.

———. (in press?), "The Syrian Euphrates as a Bronze Age Cultural Unit seen from the Point of View of Mari and Tell Hadidi." *Annales Archeologiques Arabes Syriennes.*

Franken, H.J. *Excavations at Tell Deir Alla,* Vol. I, Leiden, 1969.

———. *In Search of the Jericho Potters.* Amsterdam, 1974.

———. *Potters of a Medieval Village in the Jordan Valley.* Amsterdam, 1975.

———. "Scope of the Institute's Research Work, A short introduction." *Newsletter I Department of Pottery Technology Leiden:* 1–4, 1983.

Matthers, J. "Some Problems of the 2nd Millennium B.C.: the Middle and Late Bronze Ages." in J. Matthers (ed.), *The River Queiq and its Catchment Studies arising from the Tell Rif' at Survey 1977–79.* BAR International Series 98 II:369–402, 1981.

Figure 5.1 The Tabqa area in northwestern Syria.

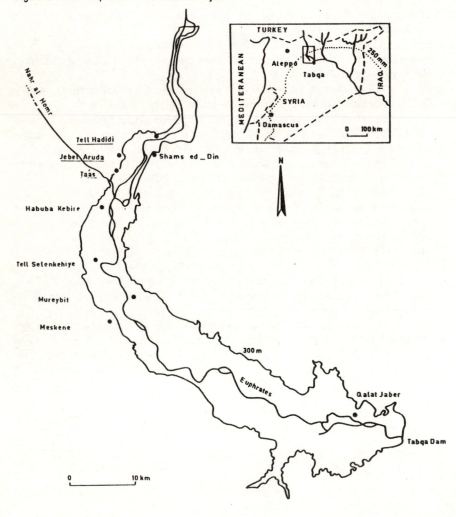

Figure 5.2 Map of Tell Hadidi, "High Tell."

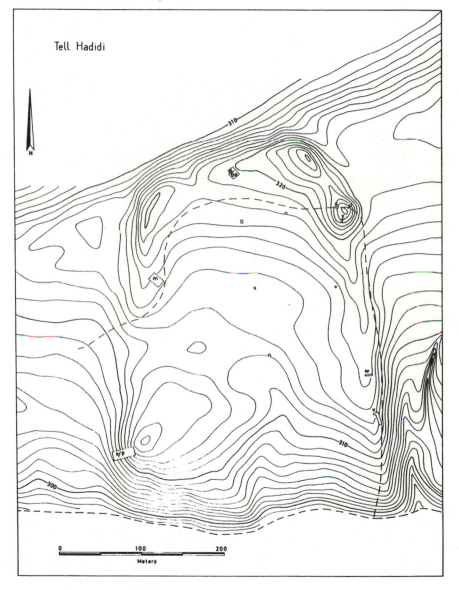

Figure 5.3 Pottery thrown from the cone.

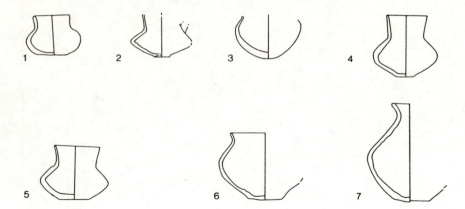

Figure 5.4 Pottery thrown from one piece of clay.

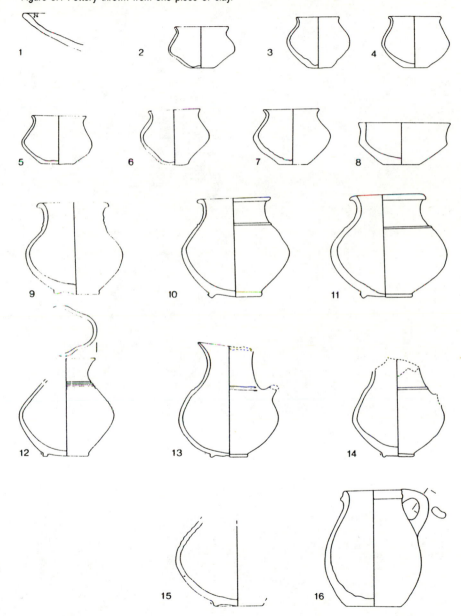

56

Figure 5.4 Pottery thrown from one piece of clay *(continued)*.

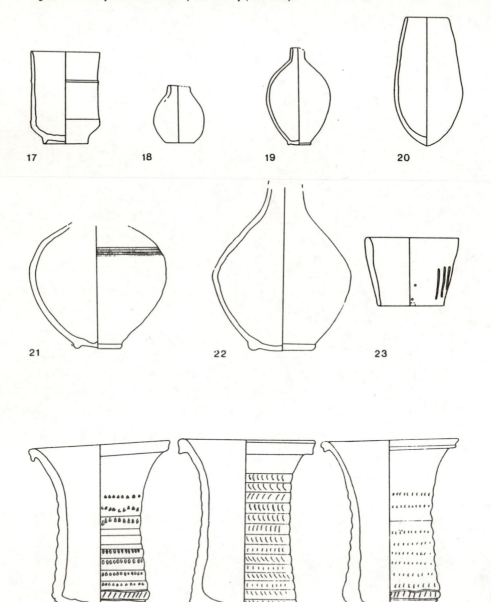

17   18   19   20

21   22   23

24   25   26

Figure 5.4 Pottery thrown from one piece of clay *(continued)*.

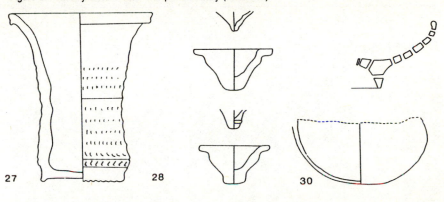

27   28   30

10 cm

Figure 5.5 Pottery that was thrown on a sand-covered support.

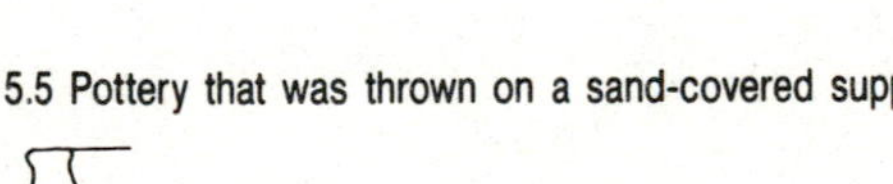

10 cm

Figure 5.6 Pottery slowly thrown in coils.

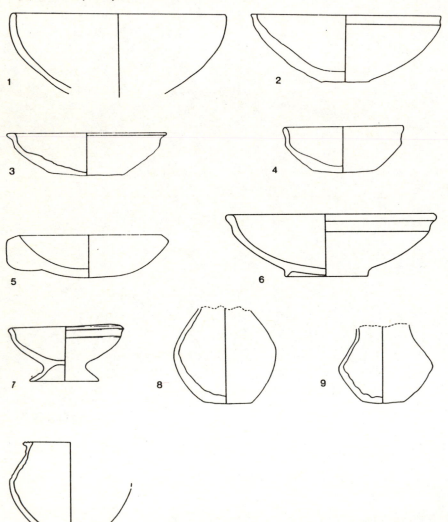

Figure 5.6 Pottery slowly thrown in coils *(continued)*.

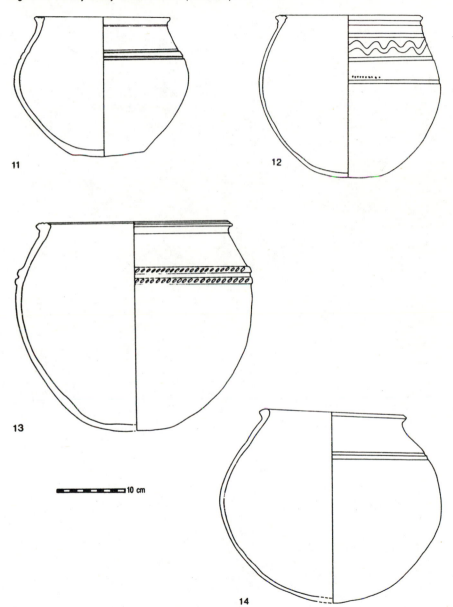

Figure 5.6 Pottery slowly thrown in coils *(continued)*.

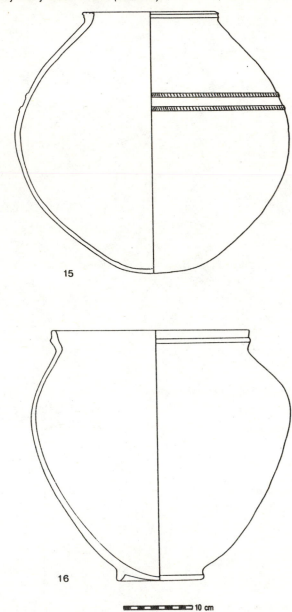

15

16

10 cm

Figure 5.6 Pottery slowly thrown in coils *(continued).*

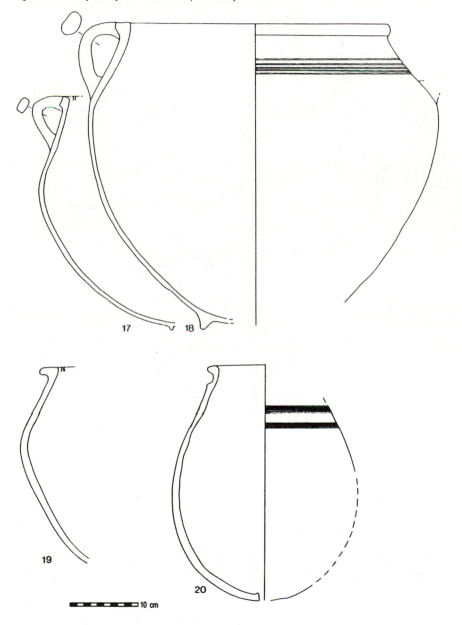

Figure 5.6 Pottery slowly thrown in coils *(continued)*.

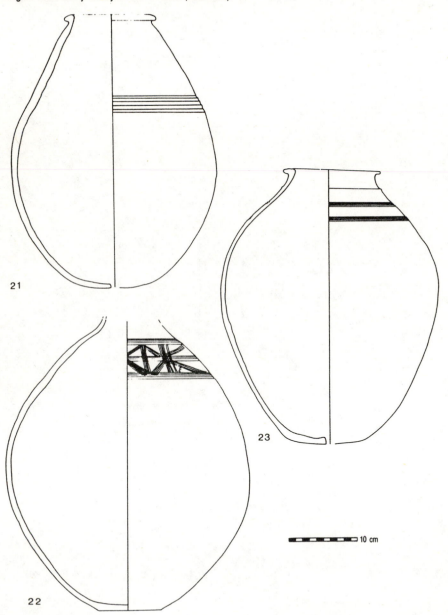

21

23

22

10 cm

Figure 5.6 Pottery slowly thrown in coils *(continued)*.

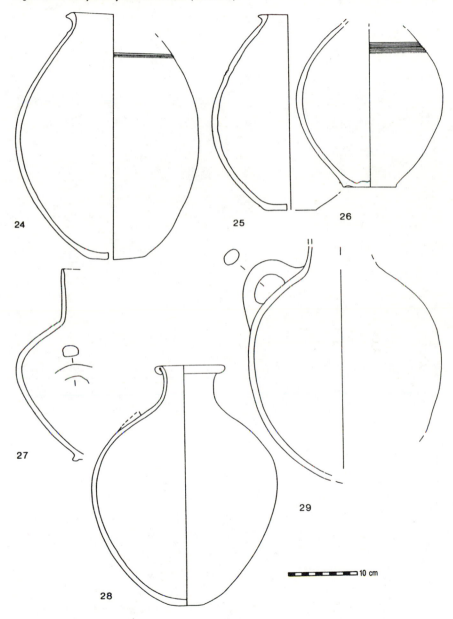

24

25

26

27

28

29

10 cm

Figure 5.6 Pottery slowly thrown in coils *(continued)*.

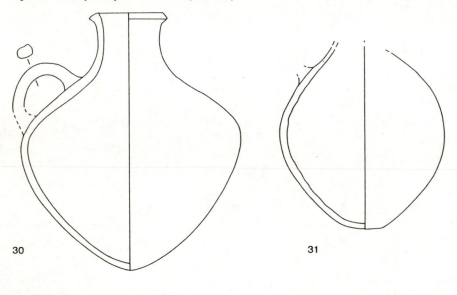

30

31

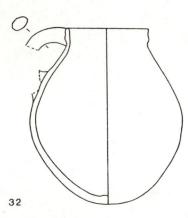

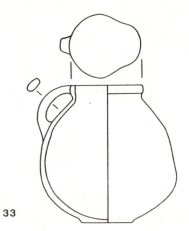

32

33

◼ ▬ ▬ ▬ ▬ ▬ ◼ 10 cm

Figure 5.6 Pottery slowly thrown in coils *(continued)*.

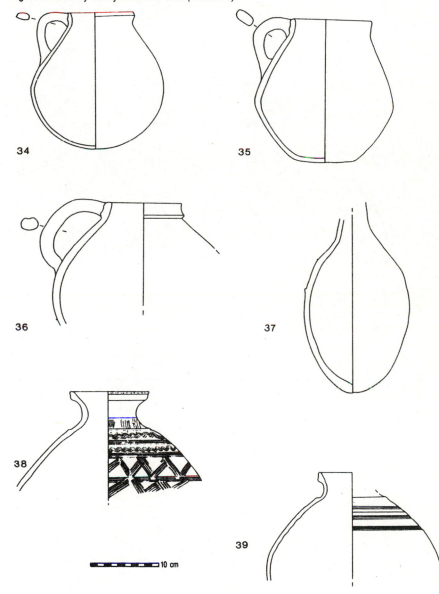

34

35

36

37

38

39

10 cm

Figure 5.6 Pottery slowly thrown in coils *(continued)*.

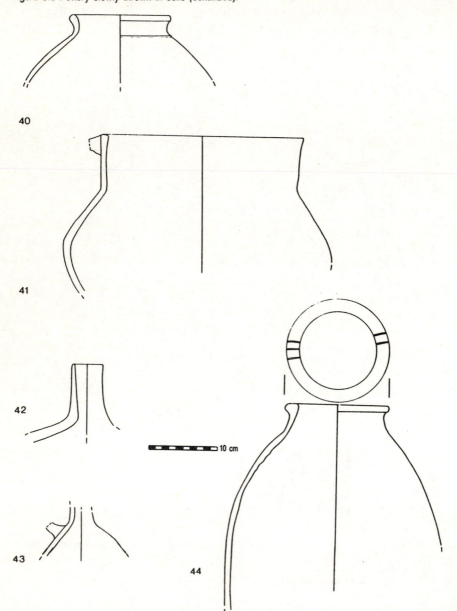

10 cm

Figure 5.6 Pottery slowly thrown in coils *(continued)*.

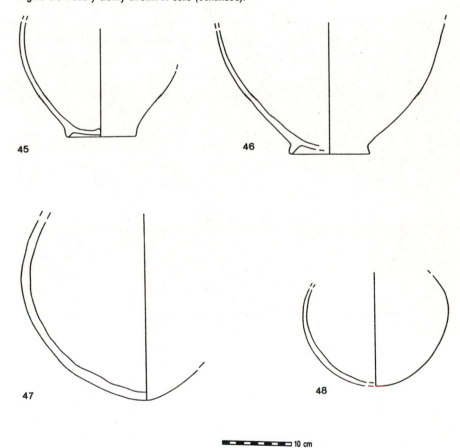

10 cm

Figure 5.6 Pottery slowly thrown in coils *(continued)*.

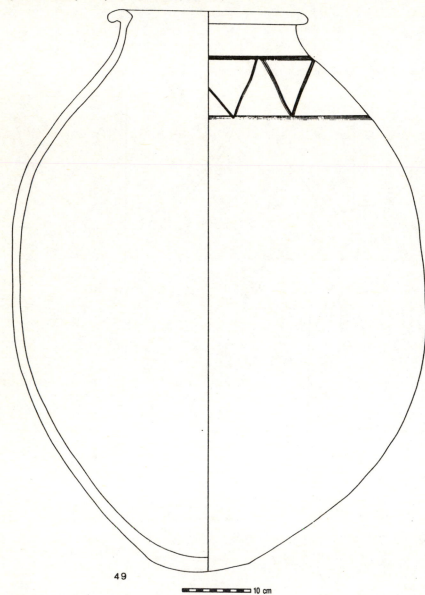

49

◼━◽◻◽◻◽◻◽◻◽◼ 10 cm

Figure 5.6 Pottery slowly thrown in coils *(continued)*.

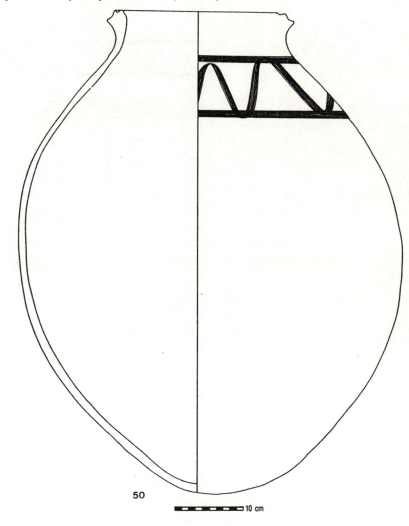

50

10 cm

Figure 5.6 Pottery slowly thrown in coils *(continued)*.

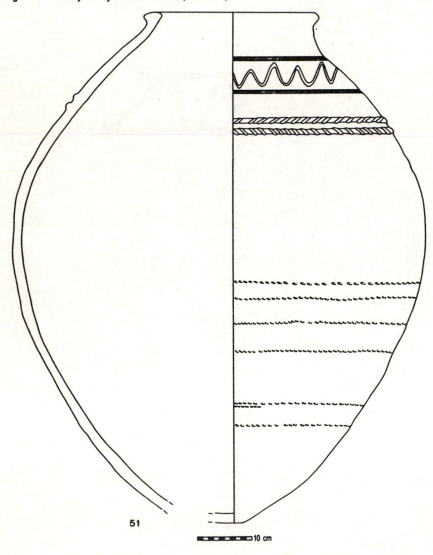

51

■■■■■■□□□□□10 cm

Figure 5.6 Pottery slowly thrown in coils *(continued).*

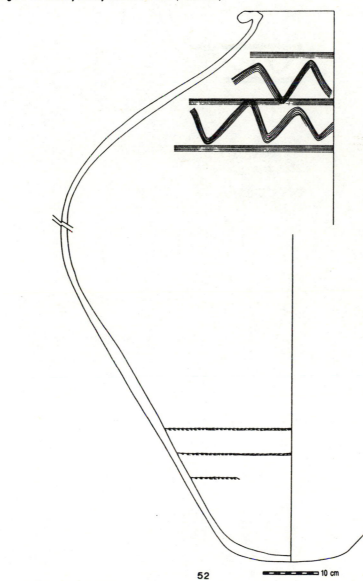

52
    10 cm

72

Figure 5.6 Pottery slowly thrown in coils *(continued)*.

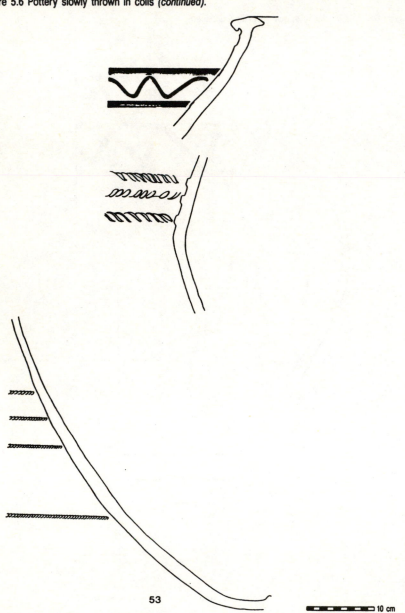

53

■■■■ ■ ■ ■ ■■ 10 cm

Figure 5.6 Pottery slowly thrown in coils *(continued)*.

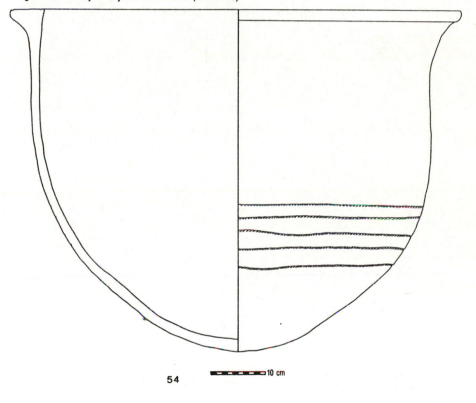

54

▬▬▬▬▬▬▭10 cm

74

Figure 5.7 Thrown and thrown closed pottery.

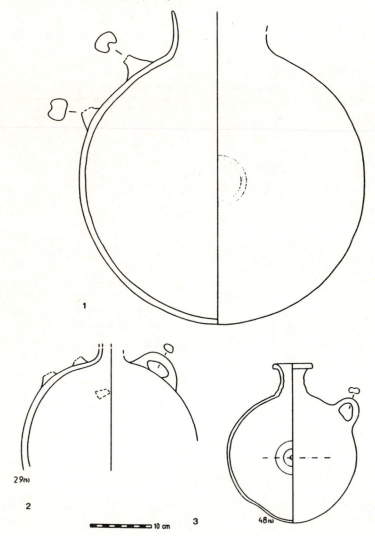

1

2

29(s)

3

48(s)

━━━ ┅ ┅ ┅ 10 cm

Figure 5.8 Handmade pottery.

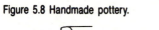

⟞ ━ ━ ━ ━ ⟝ 10 cm

Table 5.1
Reconstructed Manufacturing Techniques

	A		M		A/M	
	%	n	%	n	%	n
1. Thrown from the cone	4.4	2	9.8	5	7.3	7
2. Thrown from one piece of clay	49.0	22	15.7	8	31.3	30
3. Thrown on a sand covered support plate on the potter's wheel	—	—	2.0	1	1.0	1
4. Thrown on a slow wheel, in coils	42.2	19	68.6	35	56.3	54
5. Thrown and thrown closed	2.2	1	3.9	2	31.1	3
6. Handmade	2.2	1	—	—	1.0	1

Figure 5.9 Reconstruction of the various ways of finishing the rim.

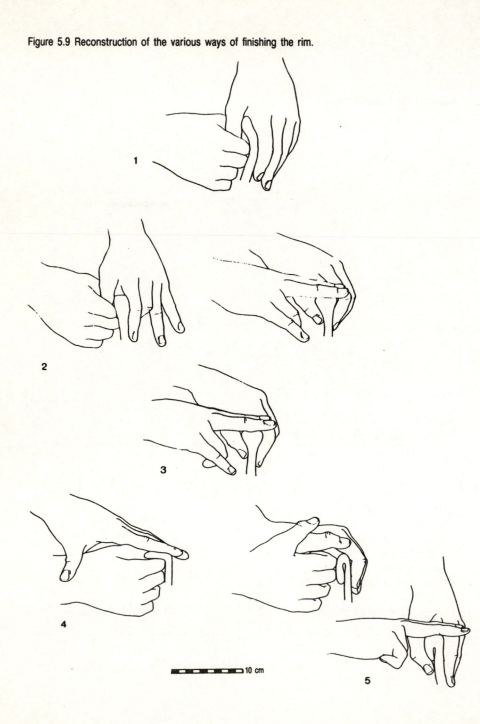

Figure 5.10 Classification of quartz grain sizes.

SAND   Grain size

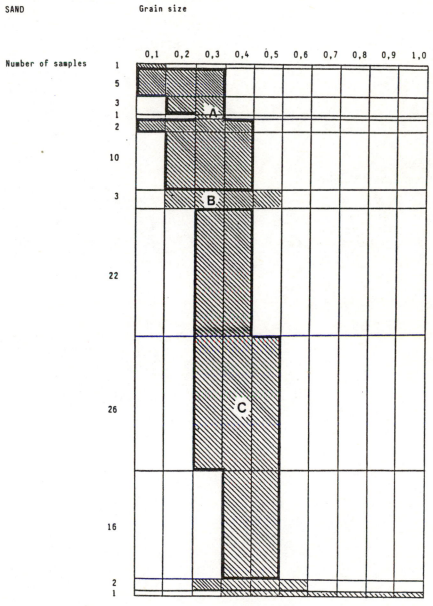

Table 5.2
Comparison of Materials

Quartz Feldspar Basalt 0.001 mm < X ≤ 0.4 mm	Microfossils			
	a none	b few	c 1%–3%	d 4%–7%
A 1 2% or less	4: 10,22	3: 6/6:30		
A 2 3%–8%	6: 21	3: 4/6: 53	5/6: 16, 33,36,54	
C 0.2 mm ≤ X ≤ 0.5 mm				
C 1 2% or less		6: 42,44,45	6: 31	
C 2 3%–8%	4: 1,11/6: 10, 20,29,35,40, 43,49	3: 2,7/4: 8, 12,15,29/6:1 11,22,26,39, 41	3: 3,5/6: 17, 19,23,25, 32,34,46, 48,52/ 7: 2	6: 5,6
C 3 9% and more		4: 17	6: 18/7:1	

Figure 5.11 Relation among shape, manufacturing technique and shape.

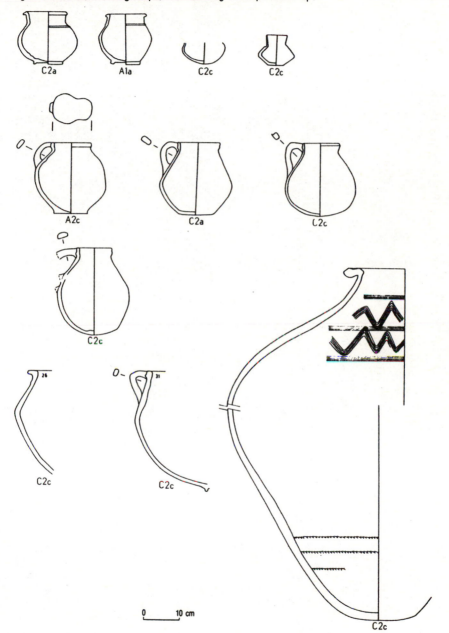

PART TWO

Production Processes

6

Thermal Expansion Measurement and the Estimation of Prehistoric Pottery Firing Temperatures

Timothy Kaiser and William Lucius

Department of Anthropology, University of Toronto

Over the last twenty years, technological studies have come to play an increasingly important role in the analysis of archaeological ceramics. Among these technological studies, the estimation of pottery firing temperatures is now seen as a critical element in the characterization of any ceramic sample. Indeed, a whole new field of study—prehistoric pyrotechnology—is suddenly respectable in archaeological circles (cf. Wertime 1973; Heimann and Franklin 1981; Wertime and Wertime 1982).

Interest in calculating the firing temperatures of prehistoric pottery stems from several sources. Being able to estimate the firing temperatures of pot sherds helps archaeologists to assess the general technological level of the potters in question; such estimates may also be useful in distinguishing between outwardly similar ceramics. Furthermore, since pottery firing involves more time, labor, and resources as temperatures increase, knowledge of the temperatures that were attained contributes to an understanding of the economics of pottery production. As well, since some behaviorally relevant physical properties, such as impact strength and abrasion resistance, vary with firing temperatures (Skibo et al. in press), estimation of pottery firing temperature assists in making

Acknowledgments: We would like to thank Ursula Franklin, Dave Lang, Steve Thorpe, Michael Tite, and Wanda Vitali for the help and advice they gave during the course of our work. Naturally, they are not responsible for the conclusions we have drawn here. Part of the research reported here was funded by a grant to the senior author by the Social Sciences and Humanities Research Council of Canada.

inferences regarding vessel function. Finally, there are times when the study of the development of ceramic pyrotechnology is an important anthropological concern in and of itself, as, for example, in archaeological contexts of incipient metallurgy (Kaiser 1984, 1987).

There are a number of ways to go about determining ceramic firing temperatures. These methods all involve the observation of changes in specific physical-chemical properties of clay as they relate to changes in temperature. In general, points of discontinuity in these properties can be linked to specific temperatures or temperature ranges up to which the pottery has been heated in the past. Heimann and Franklin (1981) mention seven properties which are useful in this regard: mineral phase, texture, elasticity, magnetism, electronic structure, porosity, and thermal expansion. This paper is concerned with the technique of temperature determination known as Thermal Expansion Measurement (TX); here we seek to discuss the advantages and disadvantages of the technique in the light of experiments conducted with late Neolithic pottery from three Vinča culture sites in Yugoslavia (Fig. 6.1).

While the use of Thermal Expansion Measurement as a means of estimating the firing temperatures of archaeological ceramics has been discussed in the pages of *Archaeometry* and elsewhere for more than twenty years, it has not been widely used in problem-oriented archaeological research (Roberts 1963; Tite 1969, 1972; Heimann and Franklin 1981; Pingarrón 1981; Kaiser 1984; Kaiser et al. 1986). There are perhaps three major reasons for the under-utilization of TX analysis: (1) archaeologists by and large are not familiar with either the principles or the equipment involved, (2) TX is most accurate when dealing with ceramics fired at relatively high temperatures, and (3) there is a suspicion that sometimes TX data are distorted by other underlying physical-chemical processes. We will deal with the first of these problems immediately and return to the others later in this chapter.

In fact, the principles and assumptions which lie behind TX are simple and straightforward. A recapitulation of these principles begins with the response of clay to heat. When a body of raw clay is heated, a series of complex changes takes place, resulting in an irreversible structural transformation of the clay. As heat is applied, water contained within the crystal structure of the clay minerals is driven off; this loss of water effectively destroys the crystal lattice. As the crystal lattices collapse, the clay begins to shrink. This process continues as, at still higher temperatures, sintering begins and the edges of the clay particles soften and then start to bond together. Simultaneously, oxidation effects chemical changes in the impurities of the clay body, notably carbon and iron compounds. The next important changes are vitrification—the formation of a glassy, liquid phase—and the crystallization of new minerals. These transformations do not occur in any neat step-like fashion, with one finishing before the next begins; instead, they overlap one another. The points at which these processes begin, their rates, and their characteristics depend very much on the particular clay minerals that are involved and the presence or absence of various fluxes. What is important to note for present purposes is that as sintering and vitrification proceed, the clay body shrinks. When the firing of the clay stops, these processes are arrested. The clay is now a piece of ceramic.

As with any solid, a piece of ceramic will expand when it is reheated. As the temperature of reheating increases, so does the expansion of the ceramic. When the temperature of reheating reaches the original firing temperature, the processes of sintering and vitrification resume and the ceramic begins to shrink. The onset of shrinkage in a ceramic sample that is being reheated is thus an approximation of the original firing temperature. That, at least, is the ideal case. With high-fired ceramics, however, there is another possibility. As the temperature of reheating passes the original firing temperature, expansion of the sample may continue at an increased rate. This may be a result of either: (1) solid-state reactions forming compounds of lower density, (2) irreversible polymorphic transformations yielding phases of lower density, or (3) the expansion of gas bubbles trapped by the surface tension of the liquid phase of the clay, producing exfoliation or even bloating (Ford 1967:62). The major point to be noted here is that when measurements of thermal expansion show a marked change in the rate of expansion (positive or negative), it may be inferred that the original firing temperature has been reached.

The device that is used to measure thermal expansion is called an extension rod dilatometer (Fig. 6.2). The dilatometer measures changes in the linear dimensions of a ceramic sample as the sample is being heated. These changes may be plotted simultaneously against changes in temperature. In the work reported here, we used dilatometers similar to that described by Roberts (1963) and by Tite (1972:298–300). Essentially, the apparatus consists of a furnace within which a sample may be suspended and monitored. A fused silica extension rod is placed so that one end engages the sample; the other end is connected to a linear voltage differential transducer. As the sample's length changes, it causes the rod to move and this movement is translated into a millivolt electrical signal by the LVD transducer. This signal is directed to an XY chart recorder which plots the expansion and contraction of the sample on its Y-axis. A thermocouple is placed next to the sample to obtain accurate readings of the sample's temperature; this data is directed to the X-axis of the chart recorder. Dilatometers come in a variety of types and are commercially available. With a modicum of difficulty, but at far less expense, they may also be constructed by the analyst. In our work, initially, we used a dilatometer built by a metallurgy graduate student at the University of Toronto; later, one of us (TK) constructed a dilatometer for subsequent experiments.

A great deal of effort has gone into exploring the relationship between the estimate of a pot's firing temperature as determined by TX and the actual firing temperature (Tite 1969; Heimann and Franklin 1981). This relationship is not necessarily straightforward. For example, as mentioned, bloating may mask the onset of resintering, thus giving an estimate that is too high; alternatively, an estimate that is too low may be the result of spurious shrinkage due to the pressure exerted by the weight of the extension rod against the sample when the viscosity of the sample in its liquid phase decreases at high temperatures (tite 1972:300). In addition, the difference between the experimentally ascertained temperature of firing and the original firing temperature is related to the differences between the experimental rate of heating and the unknown original rate of heating (Heimann and Franklin 1981:137). Clearly, care in experimental procedure and in interpretation is called for when using a dilatometer to measure thermal expansion.

Tite (1969) has proposed a simple method for determining the relationship between the temperature of experimental sintering (T_a) and the original firing temperature (T_e). The method involves first determining the temperature at which the sample sinters (T_a); the sample is allowed to cool and then reheated to a temperature some 50° C. greater than T_a. This second temperature, T'_a, is held for one hour, after which the sample again is allowed to cool. Finally, the heating process is resumed once more to get a new, higher temperature of sintering, T'_e. This second temperature of sintering relates to T'_e as the first sintering temperature relates to T_e. Thus:

(1) $T_e - T_a = T'_e - T'_a$

Solving for T_e:

(2) $T_e = T_a + (T'_e - T'_a)$

Tite's method has been shown to be accurate within a 20° C. range (Tite 1969; Heimann and Franklin 1981).

Before commencing dilatometer experiments on the archaeological samples, we gave our equipment an initial check. Tablets of raw clay were fired to 850°, 950°, and 1050° C. for one hour in an oxidizing atmosphere and were then subjected to TX analysis. The temperatures of experimental sintering (T_a) fell within a 30° range. Since equal or greater variations can occur in traditional ceramic firings (Shepard

1980:74–90), it was concluded that both the technique and the actual equipment were sufficiently precise.

The LVD transducer which measures a sample's linear expansion gives values expressed in mV. In order to determine what length 1 mV equals, a sample of 99.999% pure nickel, 0.808 cm long, was placed in the dilatometer and heated to 200° C. At this temperature, the dilatometer measured 40 mV of linear expansion on the part of the nickel sample. Since the thermal expansion coefficient of nickel is known, the actual amount of the sample's expansion could be calculated using the standard formula:

$$(3) \ L \times a \times 10^{-6} \times T = \Delta L$$

where L = sample length, a = coefficient of thermal expansion, T = temperature of sample, and ΔL = change in sample length at temperature T. Thus:

$$(4) \ 0.808 \times 13.3 \times 10^{-6} \times 200 = 0.002149.$$

Therefore, 1 mV = 0.0000537 cm.

Normally, the expansion/shrinkage of a sample in a dilatometry experiment is expressed as percent change of length or as an mV value. Precise calculations of the absolute linear dimensions of a sample at various temperatures is necessary only if one wishes to determine the sample's coefficient of thermal expansion.

In conducting the dilatometer experiments, most of the procedures suggested by Roberts (1963) were followed. Samples were first cut from a sherd, polished flat at two parallel ends, and measured. After being place din the dilatometer, they were heated at a rate of 5° per minute up to 800° C., after which the rate of heating was slowed to 1° per minute. All TX experiments were conducted in an oxidizing atmosphere.

Thermal expansion measurements were made of archaeological ceramic samples from three late Neolithic sites in Yugoslavia: Selevac, Gomolava, and Opovo. These experiments were part of the senior author's research into the organization of Balkan Neolithic pottery production and into the pyrotechnological developments leading up to the earliest copper metallurgy in Europe (Kaiser et al. 1986; Kaiser 1987, in press). The ceramics from these three sites are typical of Vinča culture pottery. Vessels are hand-built and mostly of local manufacture. They are frequently burnished and almost always fired in a reducing atmosphere. Samples were selected so as to represent the range of compositional and contextual variability within the three assemblages.

Typical expansion curves of some of these samples are presented in Figures 6.3-5. Table 6.1 gives a complete presentation of the TX results.

The profiles of the expansion curves shown in Figures 6.3-5 are not identical, but they do have certain features in common which relate to physical-chemical processes common to most pottery. Thermal expansion begins as moisture within the sample is heated and converted to steam at around 100° C. Sample dilation then continues fairly steadily until a temperature of 570°–620° C. is reached. At this point, a sharp increase in size occurs. This represents the so-called "quartz jump," where alpha-quartz is transformed into the larger beta-quartz form. In some samples, there is a final increase in the rate of expansion at around 850° C. which may, in some cases, be attributed to the transformation of calcium oxides to calcium silicates. At somewhat higher temperatures, i.e., over 900° C., the rate of expansion may also increase due to the formation of gas bubbles, low density compounds, or low density phases. Finally, there is a reversal of the expansion trend—this shrinkage is associated with the resumption of sintering or vitrification.

At this point, the furnace is shut off and the sample cools. When a sample's curve of thermal expansion on heating is not the same as its curve of thermal expansion on cooling, then it is said to exhibit thermal expansion hysteresis. Such non-coincidence may be explained by one of two hypotheses. Figure 6.6 portrays alternative models of the behavior of an anisotropic crystalline body in which the crystal grains are shown as rectangular prisms; they have a large coefficient of thermal expansion lengthwise and a small coefficient width-wise. In diagram (1), the crystal body is at room temperature. This body expands normally as it is heated, but thermal stresses create the pattern of cracking shown in (2). Some intergranular cohesion is lost and upon cooling, these grains shrink away from one another, producing the cooling curve shown in (3). Alternatively, diagram (4) shows the crystal body at sintering temperature. Greater lengthwise contraction upon cooling produces the cracking pattern shown in (5), and the cooling curve progressively decreases (6) as stresses are relieved (Ford 1967:65–66).

Overall, the original firing temperatures of these Vinča sherds—as estimated by TX—are quite high. More than 70% of the sherds analyzed here have estimated firing temperatures of 900° C. or higher. These high temperatures appear to cut across almost all fabric types. While an exegesis on the significance of these results for Balkan prehistory is not called for here (instead, cf. Kaiser 1984, 1987; Kaiser et al. 1986), it should be noted that, first of all, these data indicate that by the late Neolithic, high temperature firings had become routine operations in Balkan ceramic manufacture, and, secondly, they lend support to the theory that the pyrotechnology later used by Balkan coppersmiths was first developed by the potters of the region (Renfrew 1969; Kaiser et al. 1986).

At any rate, having obtained these results, a further question concerning accuracy confronted us. Inasmuch as the pottery under investigation was all originally fired in a reducing atmosphere, how reliable are thermal expansion measurements taken in an oxidizing atmosphere?

It is known that atmosphere has an effect on the temperature at which certain vitrification phases occur. In a reducing atmosphere, non-calcareous clays form the various vitrification microstructures at temperatures some 50° C. lower than is the case in an oxidizing atmosphere; this is due to the lower melting point of the stable crystalline phase (fayalite) which is produced by reduction. With calcareous clays, after initial vitrification, the differences are less pronounced, but are still present (Maniatis and Tite 1981:65).

To determine whether atmosphere as a confounding effect on TX measurements, a further experiment was conducted. Four reduced sherds whose sintering temperatures (T_a) were lower than 1000° C. were selected. A sample was taken from each sherd and refired to 1000° C. (T'_e) for one hour in a controlled reducing atmosphere which consisted of one part carbon dioxide to one part carbon monoxide. After this refiring, the samples were placed in the dilatometer and their sintering temperatures (T'_a) were redetermined. The results are presented in Table 6.2.

As can be seen, the differences between the sintering temperatures (T'_a) and the known refiring temperatures (T'_e) were slight. The average difference was +22.5° C. These data confirm the reliability of the dilatometer, regardless of whether the sample being measured was originally reduced or originally oxidized.

The great attraction of TX analysis is, at the same time, one of its potential drawbacks. Unlike other techniques for determining ceramic firing temperatures, it yields a relatively precise number. The potential hazard is that the temperature determined by dilatometry to be a potsherd's firing temperature may be accepted uncritically. If one considers what this temperature represents, the problem may become a little clearer.

The negative deflection recorded by a dilatometer is, of course, the point at which the sample being measured begins to shrink. To say that this shrinkage temperature is an approximation of the original firing temperature requires an assumption that may or may not be warranted. The assumption is that the sample was fired originally to at least the point of sintering. If this assumption is valid, then the number generated by the dilatometer is probably accurate. If, however, the assumption is not valid, then a different inference must be drawn. That is, in this second case, the temperature indicated by the dilatometer is the temperature beyond which firing could not have taken place. There is no way to assess the validity of this underlying assumption without recourse to other methods and other equipment.

The fastest and easiest way to determine whether or not a sherd has been fired to the point of sintering is through direct observation using a scanning electron microscope. This, in fact, was something we did with some of our samples; SEM observations made it clear that the Vinča pottery we were looking at was sintered, and in some cases, vitrified.

However, once one begins to use an SEM, there is no reason not to pursue the matter. Pioneering works by Michael Tite, Yannis Maniatis and others have shown that there are several stages in the process of ceramic vitrification, each with its won characteristic microstructure (cf. Maniatis and Tite 1981; Tite et al. 1982). Each stage corresponds to a definite temperature range which depends on (1) the presence or absence of calcium in amounts greater than 10%, and (2) the atmosphere of firing. The firing temperature of a sherd may be estimated by comparing the microstructure of a sample of the sherd as received to the microstructures of samples that have been refired to various temperatures. The temptation then is simply to use the SEM to the exclusion of all else. However, the SEM cannot provide a very high resolution. It cannot, for example, distinguish between a sherd fired to 875° C. and one fired to 1025° C. TX, on the other hand, is capable of making finer distinctions.

The use of TX analysis in determining ceramic firing temperatures does have certain advantages over other methods. Sample preparation is easy, operating costs are low, the technique is relatively simple to learn, and more precise results may be obtained. The disadvantages of TX lie primarily in the interpretation of results. For this reason, we would advocate that TX be used in tandem with another analytic technique, preferably scanning electron microscopy. Because they monitor different heat-sensitive properties, the two methods provide a check on one another, as a final example will illustrate.

One of the sherds (Selevac 600) that we ran in the dilatometer had a sintering temperature of 1055° C. The profile of the heating curve was curious, in that it exhibited a sudden increase in the rate of expansion between 900° and 1000° C. When a piece of the sherd was examined under the SEM, it appeared that while it was indeed sintered, vitrification was only in its early phase. This would suggest a firing temperature less than the 1055° C. value indicated by the dilatometer. After experimental refirings in a reducing atmosphere, the SEM showed that vitrification began to resume at about 1000° C. Referring back to the heating curve of the sample (Fig. 6.5), it seems clear that the best approach in this case would be to interpret the final flattening of the heating curve at 980° C. as the sherd's firing temperature.

In this paper, we have tried to show that archaeologists studying pottery can make good use of thermal expansion measurement, especially if this is done in conjunction with other methods which provide a clearer picture of ceramic composition and structure. It is thus possible to arrive at relatively confident estimates of the firing temperatures of prehistoric ceramics. However, it must be pointed out that, from a materials science standpoint, more basic research needs to be conducted, for the thermal dynamics of complex polycrystalline bodies such as ceramics are not yet well understood, particularly in the temperature ranges which characterize the firing of most archaeological pottery. The many vagaries of heating and cooling curves traced on a TX plot reflect the cumulative, and sometimes conflicting, responses of a ceramic's constituents to heat. Thus, there is still a wealth of information about the thermal properties of ceramics still waiting to be retrieved. In the meantime, though, the pyrotechnological analysis of pottery need not be something beyond the grasp of any archaeologist working with ceramics; rather, the challenge is to apply such techniques to appropriate problems in prehistory.

References Cited

Ford, W.F. *The Effect of Heat on Ceramics.* London: Institute of Ceramics Textbook Series 4, 1967.

Heimann, R. and Franklin U.M. "Archaeo-thermometry: the Assessment of Firing Temperatures of Ancient Ceramics." *Journal of the International Institute of Conservation–Canadian Group.* 4(2):23–45, 1981.

Kaiser, T. *Vinca Ceramics: Economic and Technological Aspects of Late Neolithic Pottery Production in Southeast Europe.* Ph.D. dissertation, University of California, Berkeley, 1984.

————. "Pottery and the Origins of European Metallurgy." *Royal Ontario Museum Archaeological Newsletter,* Series II, No. 19, 1987.

————. "Ceramic Technology." in *Selevac: A Neolithic Village in Yugoslavia,* edited by R. Tringham and D. Krstic. Los Angeles: UCLA Institute of Archaeology Press, in press.

Kaiser, T., Franklin, U.M., and Vitali, V. "Pottery and Pyrotechnology in the Late Neolithic of the Balkans." in *Proceedings of the International Archaeometry Symposium,* edited by J.S. Olin and M.J. Blackman, pp. 85–93. Washington, D.C.: Smithsonian Institution Press, 1986.

Maniatis, Y. and Tite, M. "Technological Examination of Neolithic-Bronze Age Pottery from Central and Southeast Europe and from the Near East." *Journal of Archaeological Science.* 8:59–76, 1981.

Pingarrón, L. "Determinacion de temperaturas de coccion de ceramica arquelogica por métodos dilamétricos. *Antropologia y Tecnica.* 1:31–56, 1981.

Renfrew, C. "The Autonomy of the South-east European Copper Age." *Proceedings of the Prehistoric Society.* 35:12–47, 1969.

Roberts, J. "Determination of the Firing Temperature of Ancient Ceramics by Measurement of Thermal Expansion." *Archaeometry.* 6:21–25, 1963.

Shepard, A.O. *Ceramics for the Archaeologist.* 5th edition. Washington, D.C.: Carnegie Institution of Washington, Publication 609, 1980.

Skibo, J.M., Schiffer, M.B., and Reid, K.C. "Organic Tempered Pottery: an Experimental Study." *American Antiquity.* in press.

Tite, M. "Determination of the Firing Temperature of Ancient Ceramics by Measurement of Thermal Expansion: a Reassessment." *Archaeometry.* 11:131–143, 1969.

———. *Methods of Physical Examination in Archaeology.* London: Seminar Press, 1972.

Wertime, T.A. "Pyrotechnology: Man's First Industrial Uses of Fire." *American Scientist.* 61(6):670, 1973.

Wertime, T.A. and S.F. Wertime (eds.) *Early Pyrotechnology: The Evolution of the First Fire-Using Industries.* Washington, D.C.: Smithsonian Institution Press, 1982.

Figure 6.1 Vinča sites mentioned in the text.

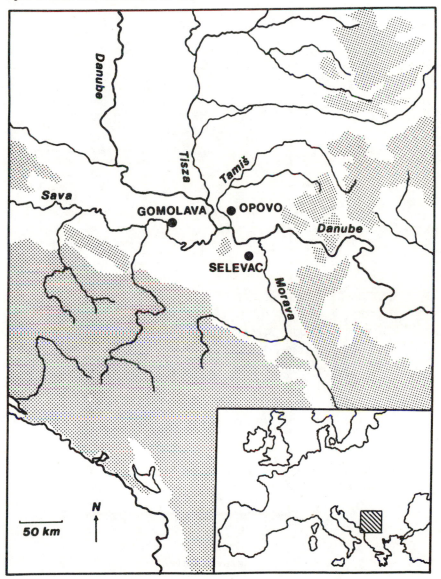

Figure 6.2 Dilatometer schematic. A: sample; B: fused silica sample holder; C: fused silica tube; D: fused silica extension rod; E: furnace; F: water-cooled plate; G: LVD transducer; H: thermocouple; I: XY chart recorder; J: belljar.

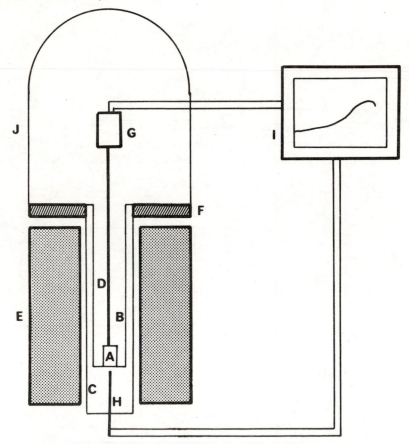

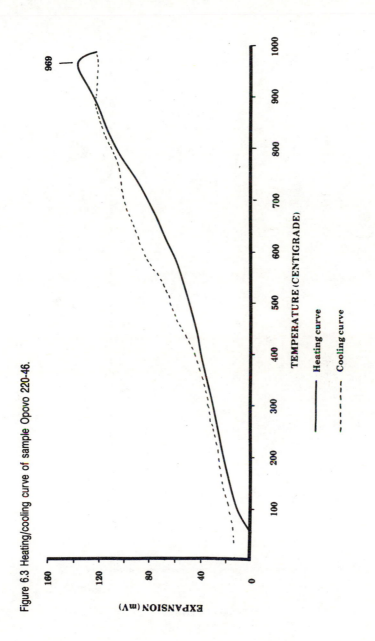

Figure 6.3 Heating/cooling curve of sample Opovo 220-46.

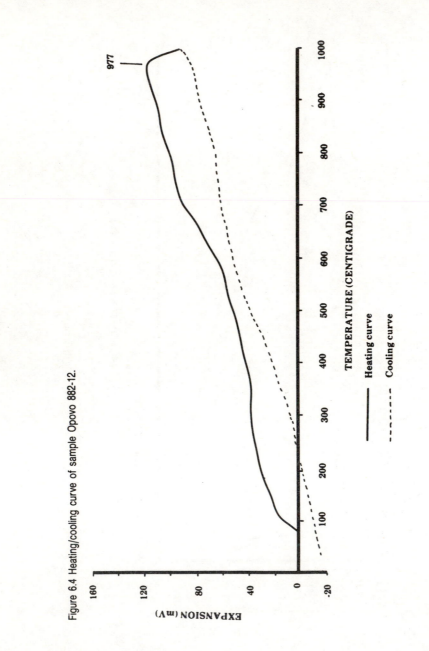

Figure 6.4 Heating/cooling curve of sample Opovo 882-12.

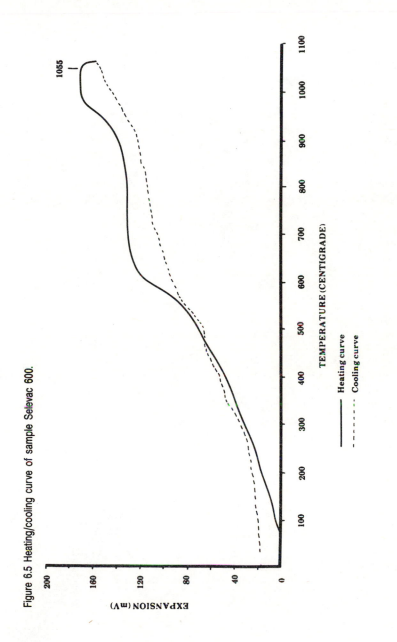

Figure 6.5 Heating/cooling curve of sample Selevac 600.

Table 6.1
TX Results for Vinča Ceramic Samples

Sample	Temper	T_a (°C)	T_e (°C)
Selevac 600	Sand	1055	1039
Selevac 613	Sand	1015	955
Selevac 627	Sand	984	1004
Selevac 628	Sand	1041	1011
Selevac 599	Untempered	1067	1043
Selevac 646	Untempered	1057	1068
Selevac 776	Untempered	884	872
Selevac 995	Untempered	1057	1041
Selevac 615	Quartz	1144	1136
Selevac 11	Steatite	850	877
Selevac 754	Schist	750	730
Selevac 751	Chaff	911	882
Gomolava 11	Grog	1000	992
Gomolava 77	Grog	837	923
Gomolava 122	Grog	1028	1044
Gomolava 150	Grog	1022	1002
Gomolava 111	Untempered	1005	990
Gomolava 16	Untempered	881	871
Gomolava 62	Untempered	857	843
Gomolava 85	Granodiorite	1100	1091
Opovo 220-46	Untempered	969	948
Opovo 882-12	Untempered	977	965
Opovo 332-13	Untempered	827	800
Opovo 330-11	Untempered	962	958
Opovo 537-5	Untempered	900	883
Opovo 96-7	Sand	880	852
Opovo 511-25	Granodiorite	1030	1012
Opovo 33-27	Grog	971	938
Opovo 135-6	Grog	1012	1005
Opovo 806-6	Grog	960	950

Figure 6.6 Two models of thermal expansion hysteresis (after Ford 1967: Fig. 31).

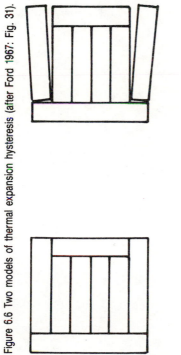

(1)

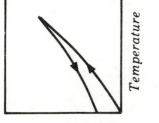

(2)

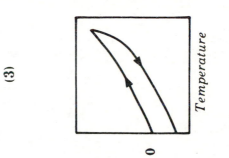

(3)

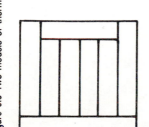

(4)

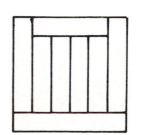

(5)

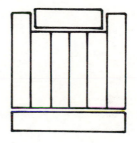

(6)

Table 6.2
TX Results for Samples Refired in a Reducing Atmosphere

Sample	T_a (°C)	T'_e (°C)	T'_a (°C)
Selevac 627	984	1000	1020
Selevac 776	884	1000	1036
Gomolava 16	881	1000	1014
Gomolava 62	857	1000	1028

7

Simple Methods of Chemical Analysis of Pottery: A Forgotten Art

Vishwas D. Gogte

Department of Archaeology,
Deccan College Research Institute, Pune, India

Abstract

A simple chemical analysis of ancient Indian pottery has been carried out which shows that the values of the ratio of ferrous to ferric and elemental carbon present in pottery can be used to classify various pottery types. The technological evolution and interrelationship between different types can also be evaluated. The firing temperature of ancient pottery is determined by studying the variation of ferric to ferrous ratio with temperature.

Introduction

With the advent of the modern physical methods of chemical analysis such as atomic absorption spectroscopy, neutron activation analysis, X-ray fluorescence spectroscopy, electron microprobe etc., a huge amount of literature on the analysis of archaeological materials started piling up. Most of these methods have been fruitfully applied in provenance studies. Mossbauer spectroscopy and scanning electron microscopy fur-

Acknowledgments: The author gratefully acknowledges the able assistance in chemical analysis by Bhaskar Deotare. Constant encouragement was given by Prof. S.B. Deo and Prof. M.K. Dhavalikar of Deccan College Post Graduate and Research Institute, Pune, India, during the experimental work. They also provided a large number of potsherds from their valuable collections.

ther contributed to the understanding of technological aspects of ceramics. All these methods have many strong points to their credit. The major weakness of most of these methods, however, lies in the fact that the analysis may not always be truly representative since the sample size is usually very small. As against this, the analyses with the classical chemical methods, although laborious and time consuming, are not only more representative but also useful in cross-checking the results obtained by the modern methods. In the present study, simple chemical analyses of ancient Indian pottery have been carried out in an attempt to revive the almost-forgotten art of using classical chemical methods.

The chemical and physical characteristics of pottery depend on the firing conditions employed in pottery making and the composition of clay. The temperature and the atmosphere of firing are important parameters which determine the course of chemical reactions in clays. During firing operation oxidaton-reduction reactions of iron, which is present in almost all clays, are governed by the firing conditions; at the end, a certain equilibrium is attained between the oxidation states of iron (ferrous and ferric). The accumulation of elemental carbon in the core of pottery is also controlled by the firing conditions. Ancient Indian pottery was, therfore, chemically analysed to evaluate the possibility of using the ratio of ferric to ferrous iron and elemental carbon in the classification of pottery types. The following five pottery types of Harappan and post-Harappan periods were selected.

1. Northern Black Polished Ware (NBPW) (Ca.600–200 B.C.): Famous for its highly lustrous surface. Grey at the core. Thin-sectioned and well-fired giving metallic ring. Main concentration in northern India but found as far away as Afghanistan.
2. Pained Grey Ware (PGW) (Ca.1100–600 B.C.): Pottery of grey colour painted with linear and dotted patterns in black. Thin-sectioned and well-fired. Main distribution in northern India.
3. Black Slip Ware (BSW) (Ca.1100–600 B.C.): Jet black in colour found alongwith PGW. Appearance similar to NBPW.
4. Black and Red Ware (B&RW) (Ca.2000 B.C.–100 A.D.): Black at the interior and the top part of the exterior. Red at the lower part of the exterior.
5. Harappan pattery (Ca.2400–1700 B.C.): Sturdy red pottery. Main concentration on either side of the Indo-Pakistan border.

Further, simple chemical analysis of potsherds fired at various temperatures has been carried out to study the variation in the ferric to ferrous ratio and its correlation with the firing temperature. Sherds of different types from the chalcolithic sites at Inamgaon and Daimabad in Maharashtra, India, were selected for analysis.

The chalcolithic site of Inamgaon (18°35'N and 74°30'N) is situated on the right bank of the river Ghod, a tributary of Bhima at a distance of about 85 km southeast of Pune, in Pune district of Maharashtra State, India (Fig.7.1). Large-scale excavations at this site conducted by the Deccan College Postgraduate and Research Institute, Pune from 1968 to 1983 uncovered an extensive settlement with three periods of occupation.

- Period III, Late Jorwe, c.1000–700 B.C.
- Period II, Early Jorwe, c.1400–1000 B.C.
- Period I, Malwa, c.1600–1400 B.C.

This extensive habitation is located on a low terrace about 14 meters above the river bed and spread over an area of five hectares. A thin cover of rich black soil occurs along the river up to its confluence with the Bhima river. The soil is very productive even with a scanty rainfall. The local black soil of Maharashtra is not reputed to make fine pots, but the Jorwe people, using the same clay with the addition of sand and other fillers, produced excellent pottery indicative of a high degree of control over clay production, wheel-based manufacturing methods and firing technique. The kiln recovered at Inamgaon (Fig. 7.2) is a huge trough shaped structure built on stone foundation. Its diameter at the top is 1.75 m with a depth of 0.70 m. At the base are several air ducts radiationg from the centre of the kiln. In the northeastern part, the kiln has an opening which is joined to the fire passage outside. This passage (1.9 m x 0.75 m) is in the form of slope and is lined with stones on either side and on top. It is, thus, an advanced type of kiln with a separate fire chamber and air ducts to serve as channels for hot gases. The kiln dates to the Early Jorwe period dated to about 1400 B.C. (Sankalia, 1974). In such a kiln, the temperature variations and gradient are relatively less than in the open air firing.

The second largest chalcolithic habitation site in Maharashtra is Daimabad (19°31'N and 74°42'E) located on the left bank of river Pravara left bank of river Pravara at a distance of about 52 km north of Ahmednagar, a district place of Maharashtra State. An occupational deposit, four meters thick, rests on black soil over the alluvial terrace. A large scale excavation was undertaken by the Archaeological Survey of India, revealing a sequence of five cultural phases.

- Phase V, Jorwe, c. 1200 B.C.
- Phase IV, Malwa, c. 1400 B.C.

- Phase III, Daimabad, c. 1500 B.C.
- Phase II, Late Harappan, c. 1800 B.C.
- Phase I, Savalda, c. 2000 B.C.

The smallest settlement dated to the Savalda occupation and the largest, the Jorwe culture, covered more than 30 hectares.

Experimental

1. To determine the total iron content of a potsherd, a small amount (about 100 mg.) of powdered sample was weighed and brought into solution by alkali fusion. It was then titrated with standard dichromate solution (Hesse, 1971). The ferrous component was determined spectophotometrically by the Fe $2+$: 1,10, phenanthroline complex formation method (Jeffery, 1970). Ferric content was determined by the difference of total iron and ferrous contents.

    Also, porosity of the potsherds was determined by the method of saturation with water as it reflects on the quality of pottery.

2. To study the variation of the ferric to ferrous ratio with firing temperature, ten potsherds from the following cultural phases from Inamgaon and Daimabad were selected.

    a. Inamgaon: Jorwe-6 and Jorwe-8 (Ca. 1400–1000 B.C.) and Malwa-13, Malwa-14 and Malwa-15 (Ca.1600–1400 B.C.)

    b. Daimabad: Jorwe-4 (Ca. 1200 B.C.), Malwa-3 (Ca. 1400 B.C.), Daimabad-10 (Ca. 1500 B.C.), Late Harappan-14 (Ca. 1700 B.C.) and Savalda-16 (Ca. 2000 B.C.)

The colour and porosity measurements of these potsherds are given in Table 7.1.

A potsherd was sectioned into about twelve pieces of approximately equal squarish size (one sq.cm). Each piece was fired at a fixed temperature in a porcelain dish for a duration of 40 minutes, in an electrically controlled furnace (12 x 12 x 30 cm). An oxidising atmosphere was created by supplying a constant amount of air through an electric vibrator. The samples were fired at various temperatures between 300° to 900° C., as shown in the Figs. 7.3 and 7.4. The potsherds were then powdered to 200 mesh size and ferric and ferrous contents were determined as above. X-ray diffraction analysis was also carried out to study mineral composition of the potsherds.

Discussion

Pottery is a result of various reactions which occur in clays during firing. The first class of reactions is dissociation and rearrangement of atoms in the clay minerals. At about 600° C., most of the minerals dehydrate completely, leaving behind the solid products which are virtually an intimate mixture of the component oxides. The second class of reactions is oxidation-reduction reactions of oxides, either formed by decomposition of clay minerals or those present in the original clay. In the present study, the analysis of oxidation states of iron in pottery was undertaken because iron is present in virtually all clays and it is most sensitive to oxidation and reduction processes taking place during firing operation. The important reactions of iron may be summarized as follows:

- $4FeO + O_2 = 2Fe_2O_3$
- $4Fe_3O_4 + O_2 = 6Fe_2O_3$
- $Fe_2O_3 + CO = 2FeO + CO_2$
- $Fe_2O_3 + C = 2FeO + CO$

A certain equilibrium between oxidised and reduced states of iron can be expected for a given set of firing conditions. Different pottery types reflect differant firing operations. For a given pottery type and culture, the potters must have repeatedly followed a certain standardized mode of firing operation. Accordingly, a particular ratio of ferrous to ferric iron can be linked to a particular ware. Elemental carbon is also sensitive to the changes in firing conditions. Thus, the values of the ratio of ferric to ferrous and carbon, taken together, should be a characteristic of only one pottery type and firing technique. The characteristic feature of different pottery types are given in Table 7.2. These results clearly show that while the Harappan pottery was manufactured with excellent oxidising conditions, highly efficient reducing conditions were achieved in the making of NBPW and PGW.

Interrelation Between NBPW and BSW

The PGW from the archaeological sites at Rupar and Jodhpura shows the same set of values (Ferrous/Ferric, % C) even though the total iron content is different. The NBPW from Rajghat also has a similar set of values but the carbon is slightly in excess. In most of the archaeological sites, BSW is usually found in association with PGW and it is strikingly similar to NBPW which is found in the later phase. The porosity of these pottery types is also similar (Table 7.2). It is, therefore, commonly thought that BSW is an intermediate step in the evolution of NBPW from PGW. The chemical analysis, however, shows that there is no similarity between BSW and NBPW or PGW in terms of firing conditions. Further, a comparision of the ferrous to ferric ratio and carbon present in PGW and NBPW, suggests that NBPW is technologically identical with PGW with a black polished slip on to its surface. Both pottery types must have been fired in highly reducing conditions at the same time and the carbon from fuel prevented from permeating the core of pottery. Taking into account their small sizes, it may be postulated that these wares were fired after sealing them in bigger earthern pots which created reducing atmosphere due to insufficient burning of carbonaceous matter present in the clay.

Present day potters of North-Western India, a region where the majority of archaeological sites of PGW, BSW and NBPW cultures are located, follow a somewhat similar method of making black polished ornamental wares. A big jar is coated with a thick paste of mud and cattle dung (Saraswati and Behura, 1966). A semi-spherical pit is dug. The fire is kindled at the centre of the pit with two layers of dung-cakes. The jar is placed in the pit and covered all around with two layers of dung-cakes up to neck of the jar and covered by a thick layer of earth and ash. The sun-dried articles are placed in the jar with a good packing of dung cake and pieces. The mouth of the jar is closed with the lid. The fire gradually developes and when the wares inside the pot glow red, the lid is opened and a few handfuls of dung pieces are thrown into the jar, briskly the lid is closed to prevent escape of any smoke. When the pot cools down the articles are removed. They will be shining jet black. These objects, however, have a close resemblence with BSW. It, therefore, follows that BSW was produced in the presence of large amount of dung cakes in the outer jar, while there absence resulted in the production of PGW.

Inverted Firing Technique of B & RW

The B & RW was analysed by cutting four sections (1 mm) of the core parallel to the surface. The innermost section was jet black, while the outermost was reddish in colour. The other two sections were of intermediate shades. The ferrous to ferric ferric ratio and carbon were higher in the innermost black section, dropping down to a very low value in the outermost red section (Table 7.2). These results confirm the inverted firing technique supposedly used in the making of B & RW. The pottery must have been fired in upside down position in closed contact with fuel creating a reducing atmosphere in the interior of the pottery with the elemental carbon possibly penetrating through the pores. The outer surface turned red as it was exposed to oxidising atmosphere. The chemical analysis shows similarity between BSW and the innermost section of B & RW. Hence, BSW, which is totally black in colour and must have been fired in close contace with fuel, as mentioned earlier, and by taking care not to allow oxygen to come in contact with the ware.

Black Polished Slip on NBPW

There is a considerable difference of opinion about the chemical nature of the black polished slip of NBPW. The black colour has been attributed to: (1) ferrous silicate (Sana Ullah, 1946), (2) magnetite (Hegde, 1962), and (3) carbon (Lal, 1960; Bhardwaj, 1979; Mitchell, 1979). Longworth and Tite (1979) have made XPS, SEM and X-ray diffraction analyses of NBPW from Kausambi and Rajgir. The XPS analysis shows 3.2% carbon in the slip. The present analysis also shows that the slip contains a relatively high carbon percentage and ferrous and ferric species are in the proportion of 90.7:9.3. From simple chemical calculations, it follows that ferrous component as present in magnetite can not be more than 4.65%, since ferric composition is only 9.30%. The rest of the ferrous species (86.05%) must be present in the form of a silicate, for at high temperatures ferrous iron immediately reacts with silica forming ferrous silicate (Searle and Grimshaw, 1960). The black colour of the slip is, therefore, a compound effect of carbon, ferrous silicate and a small amount of magnetite. The slip might have been obtained by the application of well levigated emulsion of refined clay and organic liquid (plant juices) ovedr the dried pots. After the slip was dry, the pots were fired under reducing condition. The organic matter in the slip carbonized without burning out, resulting in uniform lustrous black surface. The application of plant juices on dried pots has also been reported (Bhardwaj 1979) in the ancient Sanskrit text "Shatapatha Brahmana" (Ca. 800 B.C.).

Estimation of Ancient Firing Temperature of Pottery

Pottery fired with given set of firing conditions attains an equilibrium betweeen the ferric and ferrous states of iron. (Gogte et. al, 1982). If the pottery is refired with the same firing conditions, the ratio of ferric to ferrous is not expected to change until the earlier firing temperature is crossed. Beyond this temperature, new sets of reactions should take place disturbing the equilibrium of the oxidation states of iron attained earlier. In the present experiments, oxidising atmosphere is used for refiring the reddish pottery; the temperature where the first significant oxidation begins, has, therefore, been assigned as the ancient firing temperature of the pottery. In principle, the results should be similar to those obtained by Mossbauer spectroscopy in which the original firing temperature was detected as a change in the characteristics of Mossbauer spectrum (Cousins and Dharmawardena, 1969 and Bakas et al, 1980, Maniatis et al, 1984). However, while the chemical environment of iron can be correctly identified from Mossbauer spectroscopic studies, a more precise estimation of ferric and ferrous states of iron is obtained by the classical chemical analysis used in this study.

In the potsherds from Inamgaon, Jorwe-8, Malwa-13 and Malwa-15 the significant increase in the ratio of ferric to ferrous occurs beyond the temperatures 650° C., 575° C. and 500° C. respectively (Fig. 7.3). Jorwe-6 shows a slight reduction in the range of 600°–700° C. and a steady increase thereafter. A similar behaviour is also shown by Malwa-14 in which the reduction occurs from 500° to 600° C. and a pronounced oxidation at higher temperatures. The initial reduction as observed in these potsherds might be due to the elemental carbon present in small quantities in the core of the pottery. Since the significant oxidation begins at 700° C. in Jorwe-6 and at 600° C. in Malwa-14, the corresponding temperatures have been assigned as their ancient firing temperatures.

All the potsherds from Daimabad show the increase in the ratio within temperature range of 500° C. to 600° C. (Fig. 7.4). While Jorwe-4 and Daimabad-10 show steady increase from 500° C. and 550° C., in Malwa-3 the increase is relatively small and remains constant at the subsequent temperatures. Late Harappan-14 and Savalda-16 have shown rise in the ratio at two temperatures but the first rise in both potsherds was significant; hence, the corresponding temperatures 650° C. and 500° C., have been assigned as their ancient firing temperatures.

Further, the X-ray diffraction analysis of all the potsherds showed the presence of same pattern of minerals i.e. calcite, hematite, plasioclase (albite), orthoclase, quartz and muscovite.

This was expected since both archaeological sites are situated in the region of Deccan trap in Maharashtra, India. The analysis also showed the absence of the hydrated clay mineral, montmorillonite, which is commonly present in the clays of the region. As the hydrated clay minerals begin to decompose at 500° C. (Tite, 1972), their absence fixes the lower limit of firing temperature at 500° C. The presence of calcite fixes the upper limit of firing temperature at 750° C. when calcite starts to decompose. The XRD analysis, thus gives a range of firing temperatures (500° C.–750° C.) for all the potsherds and the chemical analysis gives the firing temperatures of the individual potsherds also in the same temperature range.

This method of estimating the ancient firing temperature can most profitably be used in the study of red pottery. However, it has been found that if the core of the pottery contains elemental carbon, the ratio of ferric to ferrous decreases at temperatures lower than 500° C. (e.g.

Jorwe-4, Daimabad-10 and Savalda-16) which leads to inconsistent results. Further, the oxidizing atmosphere is required to be carefully controlled during the refiring operation.

Conclusions

The ancient pottery types have evolved because of repeated applications of certain standardized modes of operations with the available clays. This has reflected in not only clearly distinguishable physical properties but also the chemical nature of the fired clays. Iron with its two oxidation states and carbon are found to be indicator elements in distinguishing different pottery types. It is also possible to evaluate the firing temperatures of ancient pottery by observing the changes in the oxidation states of iron in refiring experiments.

The present day sophisticated methods of analysing ceramic and related materials have many strong points to their credit. The classical chemical methods, however, remain quite useful in day to day analysis of ancient pottery, particularly when the modern equipments are not easily accessible. These methods are less expensive and with a little basic knowledge of chemical analysis, any archaeologist can undertake analysis of ancient pottery in a small laboratory.

References Cited

Bakas T.H., Gangas N.H., Sigalas I, Aitken M.J. "Mossbauer Study of Glozbel Tablet 1981b," *Archaeometry*. Vol.22, II, 69–80, 1980.

Bhardwaj, H.C. *Aspects of Ancient Indian Technology*. Motilal Banarasidas, Delhi., 74, 1979.

Cousins, D.R. and Dharmawardena, K.G. "Use of Mossbauer Spectroscopy in the Study of Ancient Pottery," Nature, 223, 732–733, 1969.

Gillies, K.J.S. and Urch, D.S. "Spectroscopic Studies of Iron and Carbon in Black Surfaced Ware," *Archaeometry*. 25, I, 29–44, 1983.

Gogte, V.D., Deotare, B.C. and Tyagi, S.K. "Classification of Pottery Types by Ferrous/Ferric Ratio and Elemental carbon in Pottery," *Bulletin of Deccan College Research Institute*. Vol. 41, 72–76, 1982.

Hegde, K.T.M. Technical studies in NBP Ware, JMS University, Baroda, XI (1): 159-161, 1962.

Hesse, P.R. *A Text Book of Soil Chemical Analysis*. John Murraya Ltd. London. 355–356, 1971.

Jeffery, P.G. *Chemical Methods of Rock Analysis*. Pergamon Press Oxford. 272–273, 1970.

Lal, B.B. *Indian Archaeology-A Review*. 120–21, 1960.

Longworth, G. and Tite, M.S. Mossbauer studies on the Nature of Red and Black Glazes on Greek and Indian Painted Ware, *J. Phys. Colloq.*, 40 (2), 460–461, 1979.

Maniatis, Y., Simopoulos, A., Jones, R.E., Karakalos, Ch., Whitbread, I.K., Williams, C.K., II, Kostikas, A. "Punic Amphoras Found at Corinth, Greece: an Investigation of Their Origin and Technology," *Journal of Field Archaeology.* Vol 11, No. 2, 210-211, 1984.

Mitchell L. Surface analysis of N.B.P.W., Dissertation, Institute of Archaeology, University of London, 1979. Sana Ullah, M. Report in the pottery of Ahichchhatra, District Bareilly U.P., by A. Ghosh and K.C. Panigrahi, Ancient India 1:58, 1948.

Sankalia, H.D. *Prehistory and Protohistory of India and Pakistan*, Deccan College Post Graduate and Research Institute, Pune, 1974.

Saraswati, B. and Behura, N.K. *Pottery Techniques in Peasant India*. Anthropological Survey of India, Calcutta, 129, 1966.

Searle, A.B. and Grimshaw, R.W. *The Chemistry and Physics of Clays and Other Ceramic Materials*. Ernest Benn Ltd, London, 3rd edition, 657, 814, 1959.

Tite, M.S. *Methods of Physical Examination in Archaeology*. Seminar press, London and New York, 323–325, 1972.

Figure 7.1 Some of the excavated Chalcolithic sites in India. Representative potsherds from these sites have been analysed by chemical methods.

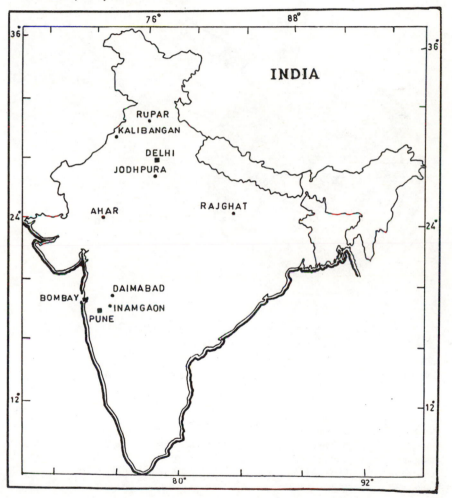

Figure 7.2 The plan of a pottery kiln excavated from the Chalcolithic site at Inamgaon.

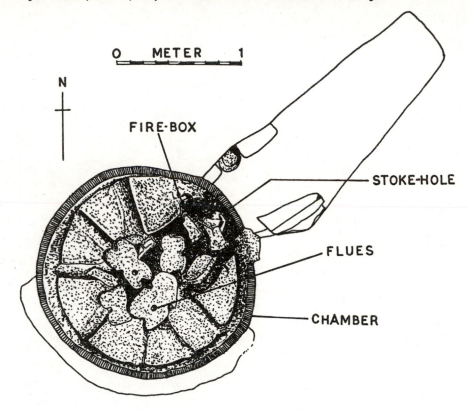

Table 7.1
Colour and Porosity of Various Pottery Types from Inamgaon and Daimabad

Site	Pottery type	Colour (Munsell Scale)	Porosity
Inamgaon	Jorwe-6	5.0 yr 5/4 reddish brown	13.5
Inamgaon	Jorwe-8	5.0 yr 5/6 yellowish red	14.9
Inamgaon	Malwa-13	2.5 yr 5/6 red	19.4
Inamgaon	Malwa-14	5.0 yr 5/4 reddish brown	19.8
Inamgaon	Malwa-15	5.0 yr 5/6 yellowish red	18.0
Daimabad	Jorwe-4	5.0 yr 5/6 yellowish red	14.6
Daimabad	Marwa-3	2.5 yr 5/6 red	18.5
Daimabad	Daimabad-10	5.0 yr 6/6 reddish yellow	18.0
Daimabad	Late Harappan-14	5.0 yr 6/6 reddish yellow	20.0
Daimabad	Savalda-16	5.0 yr 6/6 yellowish redd	16.1

Figure 7.3 Variation of ferric to ferrous ratio with temperature as observed in refiring experiments on the potsherds from Inamgaon.

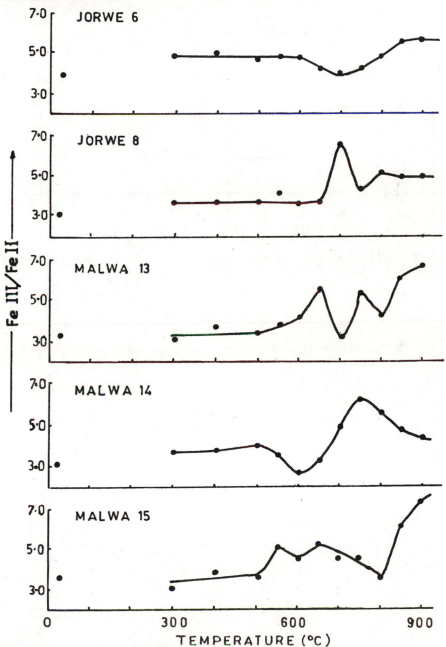

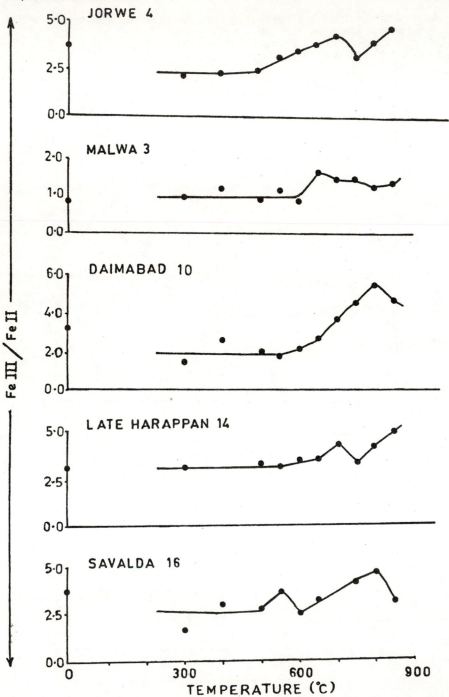

Figure 7.4 Variation of ferric to ferrous ratio with temperature as observed in refiring experiments on the potsherds from Daimabad.

Table 7.2
Results of the Ferrous to Ferric Ratio of Ancient Indian Pottery Types and Porosity Measurement

Pottery Type	Total Iron	Ratio Ferrous/Ferric	Elemental Carbon (%)	Porosity
NBPW-slip (Rajghat)	6.24	9.76	2.49	—
NBPW-core	6.48	1.82	1.39	11.00
PGW (Rupar)	6.66	1.88	0.61	14.30
PGW (Jodhpura)	6.07	1.95	0.80	12.00
BSW (Rupar)	7.33	0.59	3.08	11.10
BSW (Jodhpura)	6.15	0.35	2.60	12.60
Harappan (Kalibangan)	5.80	0.15	0.10	17.90
B & R Ware* (Ahar)				
a	6.48	0.38	2.46	—
b		0.45	2.38	—
c		0.43	1.13	—
d		0.07	0.36	—

*a, b, c, and d are four sections (1.0 mm thickness) of B & R Ware taken along its surface. Section a is innermost black and d is outermost red.

8

Trace Elements in the Porcelain of the Royal Kiln at Jiaotan

Li Hu Hou

Institute of Archaeology, Academy of Social Sciences,
Beijing, People's Republic of China

The royal kiln at Jiaotan was built in the early Song Dynasty to provide porcelain for the palace. It is located near Wuguishan (Tortoise Hill) in the southern suburb of the modern city of Hangzhou. Over the last several decades, many test excavations have been conducted and numerous potsherds recovered. Several specimens were selected for analyses of trace elements through neutron activation analysis along lines previously discussed.[1] This paper will present the results of the measurement and analysis and their archeological interpretation.

Potsherds of the Wuguishan Royal Kiln

In autumn of 1986, Zhu Bo-qian of the Institute of Archaeology of Zhejiang Province gave us six sherds produced by the Wuguishan royal kiln. Macroscopic descriptions of these sherds are presented below:

YIX–1: sherd from mouth of vase, body grey in color, about 5 mm thick, fine and hard texture; glaze greenish grey with crackling.

YIX–2: sherd from belly of vase; body greyish white in color, thin fine-textured and hard; glaze pale green and slightly deeper in color on the inner wall; thickness of glaze over 1 mm with crackling.

YIX–3: sherd from slender circular foot of basin; body deep grey with tinge of brown in color, body thin, and texture fine and hard; glaze blackish green like jade; layer of glaze thick with crackling.

YIX–4: sherd from plate; body grey in color, body thick, and texture fine and hard; glaze light-bluish grey and thick layer of glaze.

YIX–5: sherd from belly of vase; body deep grey in color, body thin and texture fine and hard; glaze outside light greyish green in color and yellowish green on inner wall, glaze layer thick on both sides.

YIX–6: sherd from unidentified vessel; location in vessel unknown; body grey in color, body very thin, and texture fine and hard; glaze greyish green in color; layer of glaze thick, external surface not smooth.

The values of the trace elements of these specimens are listed separately for the ceramic body and the glazes. Table 8.1 lists the amount of trace elements in roughcasts of the specimens. The last column in the table lists the mean amounts of trace elements of the specimens according to the formula:

$$\sigma_{m-1} = \sqrt{\frac{\sum x^2 - \frac{(\sum x)^2}{n}}{n-1}}$$

Table 8.2 lists trace elements in the glazes, and the last column presents the mean amounts of trace elements of the six specimens. The values obtained show that the amounts of trace elements in the sherds are very similar, even for those elements that are easy to dissolve, such as alkali metals. This is unusual under ordinary circumstances of manufacture.

The existence of these trace elements will not influence the quality and outward appearance of the procelain, but these same elements can be used to characterize the sherds and provide clues to their provenience. Figure 8.1 is a distribution diagram of the amount of the eight rare earth elements measured in the six specimens from the Wuguishan royal kiln. The sign ξ shows the points of the various data, the circles between them are the mean values of the six specimens and the two horizontal lines above and below indicate the range of standard deviation. Figure 8.1 indicates that all six sherds are identicial in terms of the presence and amount of rare earth elements, suggesting that these sherds were made according to the same formula as the porcelain fired in the kiln.

Samples of the glazes were obtained for analysis by scraping the body sherds. The results of the neutron activation analysis are provided in Table 8.2. The glazes are clearly different in composition from the body sherds. The contents of quite a number of trace elements in the glaze of such specimens as YIX–1 and YIX–4. There is considerable deviation from the mean of the six specimens even though the standard deviation of the glazes is considerably greater than the standard deviation of the body sherds. Figure 8.2 is a graphic diagram of the distribution of the rare earth elements in the specimens. The distribution of these elements indicates considerable composition differences when compared to the body sherds. The difference in standard deviations between the sherds and glazes suggests that the glazes were made according to several formulas and sources.

The body of a piece of procelain is like a skeleton which determines the form of the object. The glaze gives the piece of fine outward appearance; an even and beautiful glaze makes the procelain a pleasure to the eye. One of the major characteristics of the Wuguishan ceramics is the great thickness of the glaze, which is much thicker than that on the procelain from other kilns.[2] For the porcelain from the Wuguishan royal kiln, the mean thickness of the body and the glaze is less than 5 mm, with some specimens of considerable body thinness, such as specimen YIX–5, where the total thickness of the body and glaze is only 2 mm. Most extraordinarily, the thickness of the glaze layer of specimen YIX–5 is greater than that of the body of the sherd. As a result, when we tried to remove the glaze with a silicon carbide grinding wheel, complete removal of the glaze was quite difficult and it was impossible to guarantee that the body sample was free of glaze. However, it was possible to get a glaze sample free of the body of the sherd.

The colors of the glazes are greenish-grey and greenish-yellow, resembling ancient bronze or jade, as is corroborated in a number of ancient documents.[3] The trace element composition (uranium, thorium, hafnium, and tantalum) in the glaze of specimen YIX–3 and specimen YIX-4 are identical, as are the amounts of potassium and sodium as fluxing agents. However, the amounts of some common elements like iron, zinc and arsenic are very different, hence the differences in glaze colors.

The relation between the different amounts and different colors of the glazes provides a clue to guide our study. Elemental analysis reveals that the glazes on the two specimens are made of the same raw materials with the same formula; the only difference is in the use of tinting materials. This discovery also provides information about the ceramic technology of the Wuguishan royal kiln, namely that the color of the glaze is not determined during the course of kiln firing, a so-called "kiln change" in Jun ware, but is decided before firing in the kiln through the selection of tinting materials added to the basic glaze formula.

As shown in Table 8.2, the amounts of trace elements in specimens YIX–2, YIX–5 and YIX–6 are all within one standard deviation. Only one sherd, YIX–1, differs significantly. As a result, it seems there are three kinds of glazes, made from different materials. Although the methods of application and the glaze composition of these three specimens do not differ significantly, there may be some minor differences in quantity and ingredients in the glaze used for each batch of porcelain, as shown by the amounts of trace elements in the glazes.

After an overall analysis of the six specimens from the Wuguishan royal kiln, the amounts of trace elements in the sherd bodies were found to be identical and that in their glazes quite similar, showing that the six sherds were produced at the same place and time. Further, these specimens were excavated from the site of the same kiln, so it is reasonable to consider whether these trace elements could be considered typical of the Wuguishan kiln procelain.

Collected Government Kiln Potsherds

The Provincial Museum of Zhejian has given considerable support to our research work for many years and has provided us many specimens of both ceramics and bronzes. The Museum gave us five specimens from its collection of royal kiln potsherds. Macroscopic descriptions of these sherds are presented below:

^{Y}X–1: sherd from shadowy (misty) vase; roughtcast grey in color, body somewhat thick and fine and hard in texture; thin layer of greenish grey glaze.

^{Y}X–2: sherd from plate and part of mouth ring; roughcast yellowish-brown in color, body thin and texture fine and hard; glaze greyish green in color and layer of glaze thick, with crackle.

^{Y}VI–1: potsherd from bowl with decorated edge; roughcast yellowish-brown, body thin and texture fine and hard; glaze greyish-green in color, glaze layers as thick as the body.

^{Y}VI–2: potsherd from flat-mouth bowl; roughcast yellowish-brown in color, body thin, texture fine and hard; glaze dark-brown with tinge of green in color; layer of glaze as thick as body, with crackle.

^{Y}VI–3: potsherd from ring-foot bowl; decorated with patterns inside; roughcast grey in color, body thin, texture fine and hard; glaze all over both inside and outside in pea green.

The trace element analysis data from these specimens are listed in Table 8.3 (roughcasts) and Table 8.4 (glazes). Comparison of Table 8.3 with Table 8.1 indicates that the amounts of trace elements in the roughcasts of four of these five potsherds (^{Y}X–1, ^{Y}VI–1, ^{Y}VI–2, ^{Y}VI–3) agree with the corresponding values in Table 1, with only minor differences. The only specimen to differ significantly is the roughcast of specimen ^{Y}X–2, a fragment from the rim of a plate. The dotted line in Figure 8.3 represents the distribution pattern of the eight rare earth elements in the roughcasts of the specimens of the Wuguishan royal kiln; the difference between the two patterns is obvious. For example, the symbol Δ represents the value of the content of the roughcast of specimen ^{Y}X–2. It is clear that it exceeds the mean value of the content in the roughcast of the Wuguishan royal kiln and the standard deviation. The distribution of the eight rare earth elements in the roughcasts of the other four sherds essentially coincides with the solid line in Figure 8.3; on this basis, it can be concluded that the raw materials and formulae of the four specimens, ^{Y}X–1, ^{Y}VI–1, ^{Y}VI–2, ^{Y}VI–3, are basically the same as the roughcast of the Wuguishan royal kiln.

The glaze compositional analysis data of these five specimens is given in Table 8.4. The raw materials and glaze formulae of the three specimens, ^{Y}VI–1, ^{Y}VI–2 and ^{Y}VI–3, are basically the same as those of the glazes of the Wuguishan royal kiln. Careful analysis shows that ^{Y}VI–3 and ^{Y}IX–1 can be grouped into one group, and ^{Y}VI–2 and ^{Y}VI–3 can be grouped with ^{Y}IX–2, ^{Y}IX–5 and ^{Y}IX–6 into another group. Only ^{Y}X–1 and ^{Y}X–2 cannot be grouped together with the six specimens from the Wuguishan royal kiln, but the elemental content of the glazes of these two specimens are close to one another, especially in the amounts of trace elements, which are almost identical. Only barium, cobalt, zinc, and arsenic can be regarded as similar in the glazes of the two specimens, but they differ in color. This color difference may be due to the differing amounts of barium, cobalt, zinc and arsenic, which are closely related to glaze color.

Accordingly, it can be concluded that the analysis of the roughcast and glaze samples shows that at least four of the five specimens (^{Y}X–1, ^{Y}VI–1, ^{Y}VI–2, ^{Y}VI–3) came from the Wuguishan royal kiln.

Potsherds from the Royal Kiln at Longquan

For comparative study, several sherds from the Fangguan Yao (Royal Kiln at Longquan) were subjected to the same analytic methods discussed above. The specimens again were given to us by Mr. Zhu Bo-qian, who collected them at the kiln site at Wayaoyang, Xikou, Longquan county, Shejian Province. Macroscopic descriptions of these sherds are presented below:

^{Y}VIII–1: potsherd from a large circular-foot basin; the roughcast is greyish green in color, the body thin, the texture fine and hard, coated all over with yellowish-green glaze; crackling present.

^{Y}VIII–2: potsherd from a shallow cup with circular leg; roughcast in pale white color, body thin; coated all over with glaze with only the edge of the bottom uncovered; color of glaze greenish-grey; glaze layer thin; crackle present.

^{Y}VIII–3: potsherd; roughcast grey in color, body thin, texture fine and hard; greenish-grey glaze, layer of glaze thin; crackle present.

After the glaze and body were separated, trace element composition was measured and the results are listed separately in Tables 8.5 and 8.6. Table 8.5 presents the values of the amounts of elements in the body and mean of the amounts of elements in the three specimens and standard deviations are listed in the last column. The mean values are very unsatisfactory for the specimens because of the deviations in values are so great, as is clear from the numerical value of the deviation, which exceeds the mean of 20%. This is clearly beyond the range of tolerable deviations in the experiment and cannot be caused by experimental errors and can only be caused by the raw materals in the roughcasts that came from different sources and the composition of the raw materials. Figure 8.4 shows the distribution of the amounts of rare earth elements in the roughcasts of the three potsherds. Each specimen is drawn with a different symbol and a different line so that the differences among them can be shown clearly. Interestingly, although the difference among the elemental amounts was so big they were not averaged, the results of forced averaging are close to the distribution of the roughcasts from the Wuguishan royal kiln. Is this just coincidence or intentional imitation? This will take much more research to resolve.

The compositional analysis of the glazes is presented in Table 8.6. ^{Y}VIII–1 and ^{Y}VIII–2 are close to one another but ^{Y}VIII–3 is quite different. Another matter of interest is that the composition of the glaze in ^{Y}VIII–3 is similar to those from the Wuguishan royal kiln. Is this because the potters at the two kilns had learned their trade frm the same master or the disciples of the same master? It does not seem to be mere coincidence. Figure 8.5 is the distribution of the rare earths in the glazes of the three specimens. The above analysis provides information on kiln production. First, the difference in elemental composition in the roughcasts indicates that the kiln producing these specimens was not producing steadily on a large scale. Instead, it appears that the potters had been experimenting with different formulae in small batches. Secondly, the selection of raw materials was close to the products of the Wuguishan royal kiln. In trace element composition, some specimens are so close to the genuine product that they are almost impossible to differentiate. Evidently, the imitation was based on considerable investigation and study by the potters. The best explanation is that the technology came directly or indirectly from the same master. Longquan County is not far from Hangzhou and the transmission of the technology from the one region to the other was quite possible.

Conclusions

The emperors and ruling class of the Song Dynasty were lovers of ceramics and this directly affected development of the ceramic industry of the time. At first, private kilns made chinaware for the palace; gradually, special kilns were established to make such articles exclusively for the palace. The palace had a monopoly on the products of these kilns, and their wares were not even seen by the common people. As a result, the study of such objects can provide information about the palace economy. Of the three royal kilns controlled by the Song Dynasty, the location of the kiln in the capital Bianliang has been lost so that only the other two, The Xiuneisi kiln in Hangzhou and the Yue kiln, can be further studied. However, these two kilns were developed late in the Yue kiln system. Transfer of the Song Dynasty capital from Bianliang to Linan (now Hangzhou) would certainly have included the products, technology, ceramic masters and artisans to the south. Therefore, the Xiuneisi kiln in Hangzhou, which was responsible for the supply of chinaware to the palace as a royal kiln, would certainly have received the style, quality, technology and skill of the northern chinaware producers and incorporated them into their counterparts in its own products.

This event has special significance for ceramics. To explore the source of raw materials, formula and firing techniques of the chinaware from actual specimens can provide a great deal of information. The present article has presented some data on trace element composition of the chinaware. This is only a beginning, the first step of the exploration of the larger questions of manufacture and palace economy.

Neutron activation analysis is a highly efficient and sensitive method for studying trace element composition. Only plasma emission spectrum analysis (ICP) is comparable in sensitivity, but this method requires that the sample first be liquefied, requiring many chemical processes. Neutron activation analysis does not require these chemical treatments, and the entire analytical process is done with instruments that can be controlled by computer through linking. Accordingly, the method is highly efficient. The amounts of only 24 elements were provided in this article because we adopted the method of irradiation, cooling and fixed time determination. When the method of multi-irradiation, controlled cooling and variable time are used, the values for more elements can be determined. Taking the RE elements as an example, only eight of the 14 lanthanides existing in nature were measured in the chinaware here. If three kinds of irradiation, cooling and measuring had been used, the amounts of 12 lanthanides can be measured. When coupled with the isolation technique of radiochemistry, all the lanthanides can be evaluated. Thus, there will be more experimental data provided for the study of ancient chinaware.

The study of the Xiuneisi kiln in Hangzhou itself requires more work. What is its relation with the Yueyao? Does the Bianjing kiln still exist? If it exists, then what was its relationship to the other two royal kilns? If it does not exist, then is it the Hu Yao kiln in Linru County of Henan

Province or the Yue Yao kiln in the Yuhang area of Zhejiang Province? These are the problems about the three royal kilns of the Song Dynasty. There are still many other questions about the Yueyao system itself and its relation with the Xiuneisi kiln, as for instance the Ge (elder brother) Yao and Di (younger brother) Yao and their locations. What are the essential differences and similarities between the products of the Ge Yao now extand the products of the Longquan Yao? We have analyzed the Song Dynasty chinaware in the district of Anfu county in western Zhejian Province.[4] Trace element composition of sherds from Anfu differ from those of both the Wuguishan royal kiln and the Wayaoyang, Xikou. For the Song Dynasty chinaware of Shangpu and Cao'e, we went to the sites of the ancient kiln and collected sherds for analysis. The sherds of Xiaoxiantan, Jiazhang and Yaosi of Shangyu County were provided by the cultural house of the county, and they are also being analyzed. These data will be useful for further study.

The trace element composition of the ancient chinawares are the most essential in the study of ancient porcelain. Our work has just begun. The greatest difficulty has been acquisition and analysis of specimens. The products of the famous ancient kilns are considered great treasures and are not usually available for analysis. A sherd of unknown provenience is subject to dispute about its authenticity. These are the problems we met in the determination of the potsherd of the Ru Yao. Since then, we have used only ceramic specimens from excavations; for those famous ancient procelains whose production kilns have not been discovered, all the tools of research are useless in their study.

Notes

1. Li Hu Hou *et al.* "Assay of Trace Elements in Longquan Green Ware by Neutron Activation Analysis." *Journal of the Chinese Silicate Society.* 12(3), 1984.

2. Li Hu Hou *et al.* "The Trace Elements in Jun Ware." *Journal of the Chinese Silicate Society.* 14(1), 1986.

3. Ye Zhi, Tan Zhai Bi Han, *Shuo Fu* Vol. 18, *Song Dynasty.* Gao Lian, Zun Sheng Ba Jian, *Si Ku Quan Shu* Part I, *The Eclectics, Ming Dynasty.*

4. Li Hu Hou, "Trace Elements in Ancient Chinese Porcelain." *Acta Archaeologica Sinica.* No. 1, 1986.

Table 8.1
The Contents of Partial Elements in the Body of Wuguishan GuanYao (in ppm)

Element	^{Y}IX–1	^{Y}IX–2	^{Y}IX–3	^{Y}IX–4	^{Y}IX–5	^{Y}IX–6	Ave.
Na ($\times 10^4$)	0.227	0.159	0.241	0.247	0.233	0.324	0.239 ± 0.53
K ($\times 10^4$)	3.34	2.54	3.31	3.53	3.04	3.50	3.21 ± 0.37
Rb	130	121	147	146	126	173	141 ± 17
Cs	11.1	7.09	11.1	9.69	11.1	9.55	9.94 ± 1.57
Sr							
Ba	422	580	531	583	432	734	547 ± 105
Fe ($\times 10^4$)	2.24	1.20	2.97	1.51	1.82	1.87	1.94 ± 0.62
Co	4.30	4.86	5.11	2.90	2.87	3.21	4.21 ± 1.42
Ni							
Sc	19.9	14.1	16.9	15.3	17.4	1.20	14.1 ± 6.6
Ca							
Zn	52.5	38.5	39.5	40.5	24.3	31.8	37.9 ± 9.4
As	9.39	1.84	0.968	7.03	5.12	1.07	2.95 ± 2.51
Se							
Sb	0.610	0.335	1.10	2.28	1.94	1.12	1.23 ± 0.75
La	76.1	65.5	76.2	68.9	71.2	66.4	70.7 ± 4.66
Ce	141	112	136	123	132	103	125 ± 15
Pr							
Nd	59.8	48.2	55.2	56.2	55.0	50.7	54.2 ± 4.1
Sm	10.7	9.96	10.3	10.7	10.2	10.9	10.5 ± 0.36
Eu	1.99	1.90	2.26	2.10	2.12	1.94	2.05 ± 0.13
Tb	1.00	1.47	1.13	1.25	1.13	1.53	1.25 ± 0.21
Yb	3.90	4.36	4.24	4.15	3.89	4.32	4.14 ± 0.21
Lu	0.628	0.719	0.723	0.692	0.686	0.706	0.692 ± 0.01
Zr							
Hf	9.86	8.93	9.83	8.97	9.72	7.12	8.57 ± 1.31
Ta	1.84	1.65	2.13	1.80	1.81	1.66	1.82 ± 0.17
Cr	83.8	61.4	84.6	68.9	83.9	57.8	73.4 ± 12.3
W							
Th	22.5	24.7	24.0	22.6	22.7	24.6	23.5 ± 1.03
U	4.59	4.23	4.38	4.02	4.35	4.10	4.28 ± 0.21

Table 8.2
The Contents of Partial Elements in the Glaze of Wuguishan GuanYao (in ppm)

Element	$^YIX-1$	$^YIX-2$	$^YIX-3$	$^YIX-4$	$^YIX-5$	$^YIX-6$	Ave.
Na ($\times 10^4$)	0.306	0.239	0.367	0.362	0.404	0.409	0.348 ± 0.065
K ($\times 10^4$)	2.27	2.26	2.99	3.03	3.00	3.51	2.84 ± 0.49
Rb	139	131	148	165	161	174	153 ± 16
Cs	6.47	4.29	3.97	4.76	4.95	3.76	4.70 ± 0.98
Sr							
Ba	589	605	758	654	600	779	664 ± 84
Fe ($\times 10^4$)	0.840	0.552	0.787	0.680	0.709	0.620	0.698 ± 0.106
Co	2.69	2.67	3.09	2.17	2.15	2.33	2.52 ± 0.36
Ni							
Sc	6.91	4.86	3.38	4.16	4.80	2.70	4.49 ± 1.46
Ca							
Zn	116	36.2	212	432	89.4	124	168 ± 141
As	11.7	1.38	0.561	2.94	4.13	1.03	3.62 ± 4.17
Se							
Sb	0.661	0.295	0.225	0.501	0.911	0.272	0.478 ± 0.269
La	66.6	45.5	39.9	33.9	42.0	43.6	45.3 ± 11.2
Ce	103	61.1	38.0	46.5	50.0	41.4	58.3 ± 23.6
Pr							
Nd	43.2	32.7	27.9	24.8	35.0	36.1	33.3 ± 6.5
Sm	8.10	7.95	5.61	5.64	7.35	8.43	7.18 ± 1.25
Eu	1.08	1.24	0.948	0.863	0.995	1.06	1.03 ± 0.13
Tb	0.639	1.36	0.811	0.701	1.02	1.23	0.960 ± 0.293
Yb	2.14	3.75	2.43	2.59	3.04	3.61	2.93 ± 0.65
Lu	0.381	0.616	0.404	0.425	0.493	0.583	0.484 ± 0.097
Zr							
Hf	4.66	4.49	3.59	3.80	4.09	3.39	3.99 ± 0.49
Ta	1.21	1.08	1.11	1.20	1.16	1.28	1.17 ± 0.072
Cr	26.8	16.8	12.1	16.3	20.5	7.39	16.6 ± 6.7
W							
Th	18.6	20.8	18.5	18.4	18.1	20.8	19.2 ± 1.3
U	2.91	3.18	2.55	2.83	2.98	3.19	2.94 ± 0.24

Figure 8.1 Distribution of rare earth elements in the body of Wuguishan GuanYao.

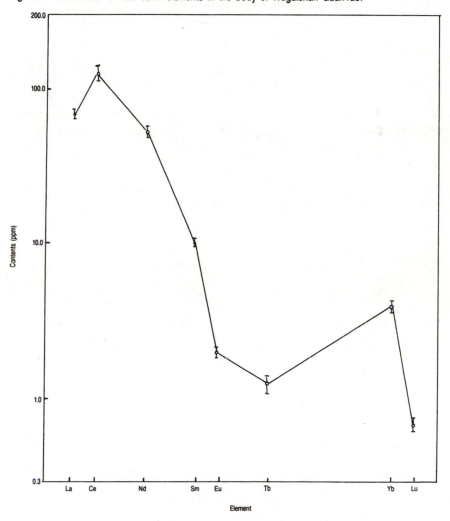

Figure 8.2 Distribution of rare earth elements in the glaze of Wuguishan GuanYao.

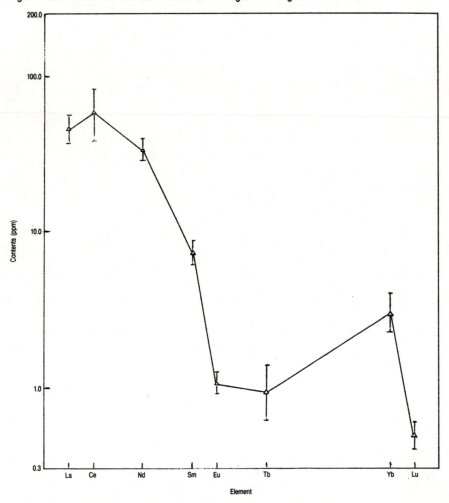

Table 8.3
The Contents of Partial Elements in the Body of Wuguishan GuanYao (in ppm)

Element	^{Y}X–1	^{Y}X–2	^{Y}VI–1	^{Y}VI–2	^{Y}VI–3
Na ($\times 10^4$)	0.802	0.141	0.137	0.154	0.611
K ($\times 10^4$)	2.76	4.36	3.20	2.39	2.30
Rb	188	282	122	108	129
Cs	4.73	5.49	8.33	9.53	10.3
Sr					
Ba	246	261	525	302	435
Fe ($\times 10^4$)	1.45	1.41	1.61	2.05	1.75
Co	3.25	2.09	5.98	6.02	4.19
Ni					
Sc	5.68	5.61	15.8	17.9	10.9
Ca					
Zn	34.9	56.8	80.1	71.7	83.1
As	1.18	—	3.79	1.03	2.57
Se	—	—			
Sb	—	—	0.671	1.14	1.73
La	86.8	39.5	73.1	69.1	71.8
Ce	112	72.6	130	136	137
Pr	—	—			
Nd	59.5	44.8	55.8	48.1	42.7
Sm	12.3	10.9	11.3	10.1	11.4
Eu	1.71	0.924	2.01	1.93	2.05
Tb	1.23	1.53	1.27	0.972	1.35
Yb	3.50	4.87	4.43	4.08	4.21
Lu	0.586	0.795	0.740	0.700	0.730
Zr					
Hf	5.34	6.53	9.28	12.4	8.46
Ta	2.02	2.74	1.79	1.96	2.08
Cr	8.07	14.7	77.9	92.2	59.8
W					
Th	33.1	44.1	25.8	23.1	26.0
U	4.78	4.02	4.30	4.53	6.78

Table 8.4
The Contents of Partial Elements in the Glaze of Wuguishan GuanYao (in ppm)

Element	$^YX-1$	$^YX-2$	$^YVI-1$	$^YVI-2$	$^YVI-3$
Na ($\times 10^4$)	0.257	0.234	0.186	0.226	0.590
K ($\times 10^4$)	2.21	3.26	2.94	2.28	1.86
Rb	150	200	142	128	114
Cs	4.13	3.82	3.97	4.31	7.38
Sr					
Ba	328	554	792	803	700
Fe ($\times 10^4$)	0.533	0.582	0.734	0.861	1.07
Co	1.88	1.06	3.68	4.83	6.70
Ni					
Sc	1.95	2.55	4.39	5.38	7.54
Ca	—	—	—	—	—
Zn	53.4	79.6	—	—	—
As	2.50	0.703	3.51	13.3	1.83
Se	—	—	—	—	—
Sb	0.464	0.309	0.444	0.625	0.725
La	25.7	28.8	53.6	42.4	65.0
Ce	32.5	39.2	65.0	69.2	107
Pr	—	—	—	—	—
Nd	17.6	25.5	37.7	35.6	42.2
Sm	3.73	4.97	10.2	7.42	8.85
Eu	0.509	0.540	1.34	1.03	1.73
Tb	0.579	0.670	1.79	1.10	0.860
Yb	1.86	2.50	4.63	3.26	2.96
Lu	0.337	0.417	0.698	0.579	0.532
Zr					
Hf	2.45	3.40	4.61	5.29	5.49
Ta	0.956	1.32	1.29	1.51	1.26
Cr	4.60	5.23	13.7	21.8	47.3
W					
Th	17.2	22.8	25.3	25.4	17.3
U	2.66	2.50	3.82	3.65	5.75

Figure 8.3 Distribution of rare earth elements in the body of Wuguishan GuanYao.

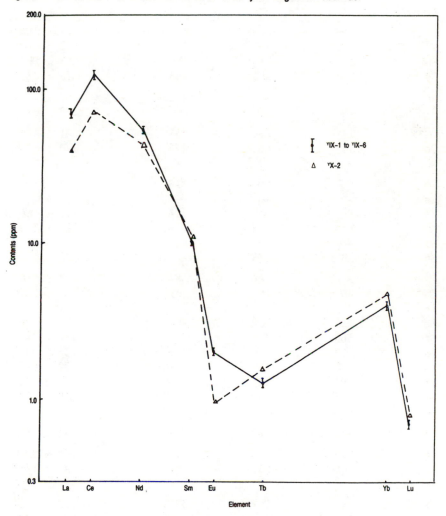

Table 8.5
The Contents of Partial Elements in the Body of Wayaoyang, Xikou, Longquan (in ppm)

Element	$^Y VIII–1$	$^Y VIII–2$	$^Y VIII–3$	Ave.
Na ($\times 10^4$)	0.189	0.209	0.120	0.173 ± 0.047
K ($\times 10^4$)	3.46	3.57	2.83	3.29 ± 0.40
Rb	246	239	123	203 ± 69
Cs	11.7	10.0	7.68	9.79 ± 2.02
Sr	—	—	—	—
Ba	619	489	567	558 ± 65
Fe ($\times 10^4$)	0.84	2.50	1.58	2.31 ± 0.65
Co	8.53	7.08	4.48	6.70 ± 2.05
Ni	—	—	—	—
Sc	11.7	11.9	13.6	12.4 ± 1.0
Ca	—	—	—	—
Zn	115	100	36.4	83.8 ± 41.7
As	8.44	2.28	0.955	3.89 ± 3.99
Se	—	—	—	—
Sb	0.815	0.682	—	0.749 ± 0.094
La	50.7	72.0	58.4	60.4 ± 10.8
Ce	107	143	103	118 ± 22
Pr				
Nd	39.6	60.2	46.2	48.7 ± 10.5
Sm	8.69	12.6	8.17	9.82 ± 2.42
Eu	1.15	1.38	1.53	1.35 ± 0.19
Tb	1.17	1.79	0.999	1.32 ± 0.42
Yb	3.68	5.05	3.82	4.18 ± 0.75
Lu	0.637	0.825	0.632	0.698 ± 0.110
Zr				
Hf	6.75	7.62	9.49	7.95 ± 1.40
Ta	2.26	2.74	1.71	2.24 ± 0.51
Cr	47.1	35.8	58.1	47 ± 11
W				
Th	35.7	50.8	22.4	36.3 ± 14.2
U	5.51	6.80	3.91	5.41 ± 1.48

Table 8.6
The Contents of Partial Elements in the Glaze of Wayaouyang, Xikou, Longquan (in ppm)

Element	^{Y}VIII–1	^{Y}VIII–2	^{Y}VIII–3	Ave.
Na ($\times 10^4$)	0.286	0.316	0.233	0.278 ± 0.042
K ($\times 10^4$)	2.6	2.50	2.53	2.54 ± 0.05
Rb	231	210	152	198 ± 41
Cs	5.77	5.60	4.26	5.21 ± 0.83
Sr				
Ba	432	238	986	549 ± 390
Fe ($\times 10^4$)	0.715	0.667	1.45	0.944 ± 0.439
Co	3.52	3.93	3.04	3.50 ± 0.45
Ni				
Sc	3.99	4.01	4.33	4.11 ± 0.19
Ca				
Zn	407	376	69.9	284 ± 186
As	10.3	2.30	1.22	4.61 ± 4.96
Se				
Sb	0.589	0.461	0.314	0.455 ± 0.138
La	18.0	18.2	34.1	23.4 ± 9.2
Ce	28.7	31.5	46.6	35.6 ± 9.6
Pr	—	—	—	—
Nd	13.6	21.5	28.9	21.3 ± 7.7
Sm	3.38	3.66	5.73	4.26 ± 1.28
Eu	0.451	0.407	0.762	0.540 ± 0.193
Tb	0.548	0.545	0.688	0.594 ± 0.082
Yb	2.58	2.47	2.57	2.54 ± 0.06
Lu	0.467	0.464	0.443	0.458 ± 0.013
Zr				
Hf	3.64	3.67	4.22	3.84 ± 0.33
Ta	1.93	1.75	1.44	1.71 ± 0.25
Cr	17.4	9.45	13.4	13.4 ± 4.0
W	—	—	—	—
Th	22.8	24.3	21.1	22.7 ± 1.6
U	3.30	3.58	2.79	3.22 ± 0.40

Figure 8.4 Distribution of rare earth elements in the body of Wayaoyang, Xikou, Longquan.

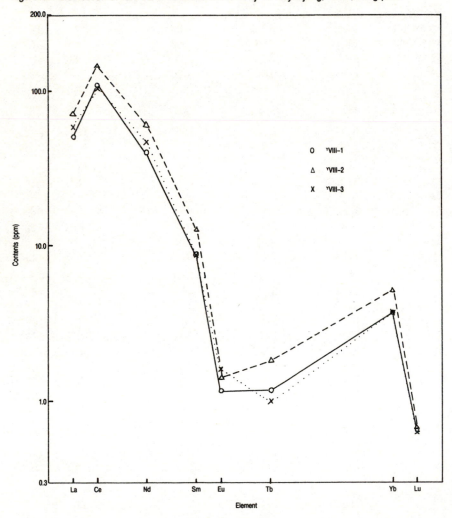

Figure 8.5 Distribution of rare earth elements in the glaze of Wayaoyang, Xikou, Longquan.

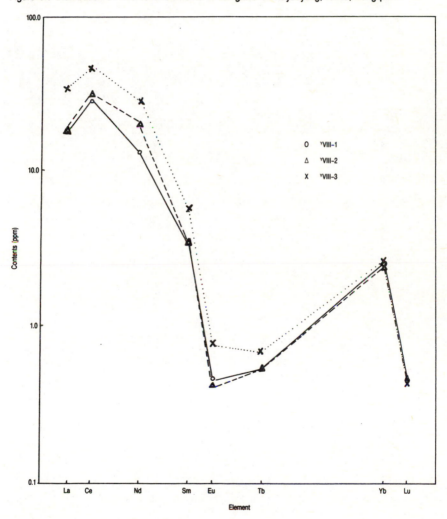

PART THREE

Ceramic Technology
and Socioeconomic Systems

9

Clays to Artifacts: Resource Selection in African Early Iron Age Iron-Making Technologies

S. Terry Childs

Center for Materials Research in Archaeology and Ethnology,
Massachusetts Institute of Technology

Introduction

The Early Iron Age iron smelting technology in the Kagera region of Tanzania, East Africa (Figure 9.1) depended upon clay objects and clay structures to yield a successful iron product. The high temperatures and reducing atmosphere necessary to smelt iron metal from ore were attained and maintained in furnaces made of bricks (Figure 9.2), lined with clay (Figure 9.3) and fitted with clay tuyeres or blowpipes (Figure 9.4).

The minimum temperature required to smelt iron in ideal circumstances is 1150° C. (Tylecote 1976). A variety of factors, such as conduction through the furnace wall, contribute to heat loss so higher temperatures are necessary to operate the furnace. Pyrometers recently used to monitor iron smelting by the Haya, who reside in the Kagera region, show that temperatures higher than 1700° C. are achieved in the central blast zone (Schmidt and Avery 1978; Avery and Schmidt 1979). Success in attaining these temperatures is directly related to construction of relatively airtight, structurally stable furnaces and to the use of tuyeres. These long pipes are placed inside the furnace with the exception of their flared ends which are situated outside the furnace wall. Bellows, placed at the flared ends, propel air through the pipes into the furnace center to stimulate and maintain combustion. The heat enveloping the pipes inside the furnace, in tandem with a punctuated bellowing motion, preheats the pumped air as it passes through the tuyeres. When this preheated air emerges at the periphery of the blast zone, it raises the operating temperature of the smelt to well above the minimum required (Avery and Schmidt 1979; Childs and Schmidt 1985). Simultaneously, the tuyere tips are subjected to extreme thermal conditions (Figure 9.4).

The ceramic objects and materials used in iron smelting must be sufficiently refractory to remain structurally stable, without deformation or failure, for prolonged periods at high temperatures. The tuyere clays must also be plastic and workable enough to form the long pipes without crumbling, breaking or collapse. Excavations of Early Iron Age furnaces in the Kagera region which contain numerous furnace bricks, furnace pit liners and tuyeres indicate that appropriate clays were available and successfully used by the ancient iron smelters. Macroscopic inspection of these objects has suggested that different clays were used for different functions in the smelting process and, of these various clays, some had to be specially prepared. In particular, the excavated tuyeres, unlike the bricks and liners, were found to contain broken sherd inclusions.

The extreme conditions of high-temperature iron smelting suggests that specialized clays might be required. The observed variability among the clay objects used in prehistoric iron smelting implies that clay selection involved careful decision-making, but the range of choices is unknown. A useful way to begin understanding that selection process and its ramifications for ancient technology is to investigate the range of modern clays available in the Kagera region, their physical variation, and their functional suitability. A idea of this range of variation might suggest the criteria by which the ancient craftsmen selected clays for specific functions, why clay preparation seemed to be required for some clays and not others, and whether compromises were made between clay resource accessibility and its performance during use. All these considerations, whether in prehistory or the present-day, involve understanding and working with the requirements of iron smelting and the limitations of available clay-based resources.

This paper presents the fieldwork involved in collecting modern clays local to the Kagera region and the laboratory experiments used to test their performance under firing conditions typical of iron smelting. The firing behavior is of particular interest because the survival of the clays under severe thermal and atmospheric conditions ultimately determines the success of an iron smelt. Considerable testing has also been done on the raw clays to maximize our understanding of how the sampled clays vary, but also to correlate pre-fired physical attributes with firing reactions. By observing how different types of local raw clays react under simulated smelting conditions, we can begin to identify some of the determinants which were involved in ancient resource selection, clay manipulation and artifact formation. Such close comparisons are possible by using the same methods of examination and techniques of sample preparation on samples of the modern clays as those used on the prehistoric objects. For example, interpretations of ancient furnace conditions are possible by experimenting with the local clays under defined conditions. The resulting physical attributes on the test briquettes can be compared to similar attributes on the artifacts.

The interweaving of techniques used here and the kinds of questions asked are appropriate for all kinds of ceramics. Most methods discussed in this paper have been established by a number of scholars (Shepard 1965; Arnold 1971, 1975; Matson 1971; Rice 1978; Rye 1981). This paper, however, is a unique attempt to apply such an approach to refractories associated with ancient African iron smelting.

Methods

Fieldwork

The field program involved collecting clays local to the Kagera region that might have been similar to those available to the Early Iron Age iron smelters. Although erosional processes over the last 2000 years may have eliminated particular clay sites or somewhat altered local topography, the goal was to identify and study general types of clays, their variability, and their relations to technological decision-making, not to locate the prehistoric clay sites. It was assumed that the same kinds of clay sources and types of clay were present then as now.

The Kagera region is topographically diverse, comprising several zones that are used in different ways and provide different kinds of resources to the inhabitants. The principal topographical zones in the area of concentrated Early Iron Age occupation are: the coast of Lake Victoria where only small village pockets now exist; the unoccupied swamplands which border several river systems and include many inundated valleys; and, the ridges and their sides that rise above and parallel to many of the swamps. The majority of past and present human activity has occurred in this latter zone. In order to assess the distribution of clay resources for iron smelting in this part of the region, it was essential to sample a variety of clays or clay-based materials from these topographical zones (Figure 9.5).

Since modern Haya iron smelters do not build furnaces out of bricks, attention was directed toward the modern brick clays used to construct houses and other structures. Although these materials do not need to withstand high temperatures, as did the clays used to make furnace bricks, both must meet the basic requirements for architectural stability. These modern resources, usually sandy in texture and lacking plasticity, were collected from upper banks along the edges of swamps (BC-1, R-

1, L-1)[1] or on the tops and flanks of the ridges above the swamps (K-1, N-1). Such tropical soils are in relatively early stages of breakdown, so they tend to contain iron and other impurities and to be gritty in texture.

Another potential source of furnace materials are termite mounds, an exceedingly accessible resource found aboveground in all the topographical zones of the region. Since the clay and sand components of the mounds are well-mixed and sorted by the termites during construction (Hesse 1955), they are easy to form when damp. Termite mounds are used by the Haya iron workers (Schmidt & Avery 1978), along with many other African iron smelting groups (Cline 1937), to build and line furnaces. Samples were taken near swamps (BB-2, RW-2), from an archaeological site located on a sandstone ridge (KM-2), and from a fossilized beach of Lake Victoria (KA-2). A sharp iron tool was usually needed to break into a mound's hard exterior shell in order to expose the moist, fine-grained, interior passageways (Figure 9.6). The sub-soils that the termites carry to the surface are similar to the brick clays since they come from essentially the same topographical sources.

Lastly, the modern clays potentially most similar to those clays used to make prehistoric smelting tuyeres include those for: smelting tuyeres; forging tuyeres which are involved in making tools from smelted iron at lower temperatures than smelting; and, pottery. While there is no reason to assume that pottery clays have the physical make-up to survive a smelt, the possiblity that some might be useful as refractories could not be dismissed without testing.

The tuyere and pottery clays were always found in swamps (BC-3, KW-3, R-3, RW-3, L-3, KY-3) or in small bogs that had streams running through them (KK-3, KO-3). The wet context of swamplands means that the clays can be readily tested for their texture and plasticity, the primary criteria used by the informants to identify good tuyere or pottery clays. These materials sometimes contained small lumps of blueish, very fine-grained clay which lacked plasticity.

These various types of clays were located by interviewing former iron smelters, modern brick makers and practicing potters. Each man was then transported to the site of his preferred clay. Sampling was done with a bucket auger which could penetrate most soils to two meters. As soil and clay layers were brought up, they were tested by the informant. When one was identified for a particular function, approximately one kilogram was collected for laboratory testing. Notes were taken on its depth, physical characteristics and surrounding clay layers (Childs 1986). Twenty-three clays were sampled in total but, because multiple samples from a few sites proved to be very similar, only the twenty unique samples are reported here.

Laboratory Analyses

Laboratory tests were used to assess the physical variation of the clay samples in their raw state and after they were fired in conditions approximating those of a smelt. The former tests were done as each clay was made into a series of $3 \times 1 \times 3/8''$ test tiles, while the latter experiments used $1''$ square briquettes cut from the test tiles. Designing the firing experiments involved considering the kinds of conditions to which the different artifact classes were subjected during an iron smelt.

Since the principal atmosphere maintained within a successful iron smelting furnace is a reducing one, the interior of a furnace brick wall and the pit liner are primarily reduced over a wide range of temperatures (600-1200° C.). Air can leak in through cracks between bricks and at the tuyere holes, leaving some brick ends oxidized. The brick exteriors are fully oxidized and probably reach around 100-200° C. from furnace heat conducted through the clay. The tuyeres are also subjected to a variety of temperatures and atmospheres (Figure 9.4). Their tips and interiors are oxidized as air passes through the pipe and out around the tip into the furnace center (Avery & Schmidt 1979:Figure 9.7). These oxidized tips also experience the highest temperatures of a smelt since they sit at the edge of the blast zone. Behind the tips, the pipe exteriors are subjected to the reducing atmosphere of the smelt and to temperatures that decrease toward the furnace wall. The firing experiments, then, had to be designed to replicate the variations in temperature, atmosphere and time involved in smelting iron in this type of furnace.

The devised experimental firing schedule replicated a Haya iron smelt which had been recently documented (Schmidt and Avery 1978; Avery and Schmidt 1979). The initial 40 minute period of heating at 250° C. represented the final drying phase for the furnace clays, as well as some time for roasting iron ore. This was followed by a rapid temperature rise at a rate of 25° C. per minute following the documented curve of a typical experimental iron smelt (#15) performed by Tylecote et al. (1971). This phase took 20–50 minutes, depending on the final temperature attained. The longest phase of the firing schedule was a 3.5–4 hour soaking period at the desired maximum temperature. The final phase of the schedule was a three hour cooling period which made the total firing time about eight hours. The temperature intervals tested were 600, 800, 1000, 1200, 1400 and 1500° C. This schedule was used under both oxidizing and reducing (using a 1:1 ratio of $CO:CO_2$) atmospheres, except that the 600° C. temperature interval was only conducted in a reducing atmosphere.

A final consideration in the experimental design was to replicate an important attribute which distinguished the ancient tuyeres and pottery from the furnace bricks and liners. This is the addition of broken sherd or grog inclusions to the former clays. Present-day Haya tuyere makers and potters continue to add nonplastics to their clays because they believe it insures against cracking during drying and firing. To test whether the addition of nonplastics improves the functioning of the clays, two series of test tiles were made for the tuyere and pottery clay samples. Approximately 17% by weight of commercial grog temper was added to one set of tiles while the other set was not altered. The percentage of nonplastics added was determined by point counting the relative amounts of clay, inclusions and voids on thin sections of several Early Iron Age tuyere and pot sherds.

After each firing under a different thermal and atmospheric condition, a number of physical tests were performed on each briquette to examine the performance and range of variability of the samples. The tests included: Mohs' hardness; Munsell color; linear firing shrinkage; apparent absorption; and apparent porosity. Macroscopic and petrographic examinations provided the evidence for cracking, spalling, bloating and melting, along with thermal alterations of the natural and purposely added inclusions. Chemical analysis by electron probe microscopy was also performed on the thin sections made from the briquettes (Childs 1986).

Most of these tests and analytical techniques were chosen because they could be performed on the ancient artifacts. This permits fairly direct comparisons between the thermal and atmospheric reactions of the clay briquettes and the excavated artifacts. Some allowance for differences between the sizes and shapes of the artifacts and briquettes, as well as for the better control over the experimental firing conditions, must be made during such comparisons.

Results of the Firing Experiments

There are three primary observations from the firing experiments and subsequent physical tests. First, the atmospheric condition under which the clays are fired significantly effects the temperature at which they lose their structural strength. A reducing atmosphere can cause damage to clays at 600-800° C. and often initiates serious deformation, such as bloating and melting, at lower temperatures than an oxidizing atmosphere. Second, the purposeful addition of nonplastics is beneficial since it generally inhibits the commencement of bloating and melting. Third, there is a relatively wide range of temperatures at which the various clays bloat, melt and blow apart or spall. This range of variation is seen within the functional clay groups and suggests some important differences in the local sources of clays and their accessibility.

Atmosphere, Temperature, and the Range of Reactions

Tables 9.1, 9.2 and 9.3 demonstrate the significant effect of a reducing atmosphere on the structural integrity of many clays at both the low and high ends of the temperature scale. Spalling and cracking on the briquette surfaces for one third of the tested clays occur at 600° C. and occasionally at 800° C. Surface spalling is always associated with the growth of carbon deposits under the clay surface. Excessive deposits throughout the paste can cause additional stresses which result in severe cracking and eventual disintegration such as occurred for sample RW-2, a termite mound sample (Figure 9.7).

Industrial ceramists focused on this problem in the first half of this century when a number of brick-lined blast furnaces suffered from premature disintegration (Furnas 1936; Rigby, Booth & Green 1944; Clews, Ball & Green 1946). They found that the deposition of carbon in the pastes is caused by the dissociation of carbon monoxide into carbon and carbon dioxide in a reducing atmosphere between 500-800° C. The presence of iron oxides acts as a catalyst for carbon deposition which builds up until the brick completely disintegrates. The amount of iron oxide in a clay, however, does not seem to be a significant factor in how much carbon is deposited (Furnas 1936).

The bricks and pit liners in the Early Iron Age smelting furnaces were subjected to a variety of temperatures in relation to their position on the structure. The coolest temperatures exist at the uppermost region of the furnace stack where the bricks, if made of a susceptible clay, could have suffered the effects of CO dissociation and carbon build-up. Table 1 shows that not all of the brick and termite mound materials are susceptible to this problem, however. It is also possible that the reduced ends of the tuyeres closest to the furnace wall (where relatively lower temperatures prevail) might have been affected by the carbon build-up and spalling phenomenon. Table 9.2 reveals that only a few of the tuyere and pottery clay briquettes develop this condition and, of those, none break apart. This is important since the briquettes are somewhat thinner than the average thickness of a tuyere wall so it is unlikely that this problem would have severely damaged the tuyeres.

At the upper end of the temperature scale, many of the clays develop the structural problems of bloating (Figure 9.8) and melting at lower temperatures in a reducing atmosphere than in an oxidizing one (Tables 9.1, 9.2 and 9.3). The iron oxides (Fe_2O_3) in the clays become reduced to FeO, an active flux. Fluxing by FeO begins at 900° C. and initiates sintering and melting (Hamer 1975:37–38). Any other volatile oxides trapped in the melt may give off gases which then cause bloating as the gases attempt to escape through the viscous material.

The brick and termite mound samples, if used for furnace construction, need to be resistant to structural failure at high temperatures in a reducing atmosphere. Several of the samples are only structurally stable to 1200° C., near the minimum smelting temperature, before bloating or melting occurs (Table 9.1). This does not mean that such materials, when incorporated into a furnace structure, are necessarily incapable of surviving an iron smelt. Only an estimated 15-20% of the furnace wall, in an area surrounding the blast zone, is subjected to critically high temperatures. Even in this area, the extent of the damage depends upon the thickness of the wall. The inner surface of the wall is subjected to the highest temperatures, while a thermal gradient through the remaining thickness insures decreasingly severe effects (Figure 9.2).

The Early Iron Age furnace bricks are typically 6–8 cm. thick. The most telling indication of a significant thermal gradient between their interior and exterior surfaces is a clear, sometimes dramatic, change in hardness. When the series of fired briquettes are compared with various parts of the ancient bricks, similar physical reactions can be identified and related to specific firing conditions. The comparative evidence testifies that only some bricks were subjected to high temperatures, most likely those around the blast zone, and only 1–2 cms. of their interior faces were actually affected. The reactions from the 1200° C., reducing firing are the closest to the high temperature brick reactions based on color, hardness and surface reactions. Since only the interior surfaces of some brick courses were affected by high temperatures, the majority of the furnace was probably left in a stable condition.

It is crucial that the tuyere tips survive the highest temperatures of a smelt in an oxidizing atmosphere, which exits from and envelops the tip, without drastic structural alteration. Any melting or bloating which causes the tip to collapse obstructs the flow of preheated air into the furnace. Such deformation reduces the operating temperatures of a smelt and limits iron production. Table 9.3 shows that most of the tested tuyere and pottery clays are effective up to and often above 1500° C. in an oxidizing atmosphere. Clay KO-3, in contrast, is a montmorillonite clay with poorer refractory properties than the others. Clay B-4, a pottery clay, and clay R-3 are the most refractory and durable (do not crack during drying or firing) clays of all those collected. Tuyere clay RW-3 is also very refractory but cracks somewhat during drying.

The extreme effects produced under a reducing atmosphere should not be a problem at the tuyere tips. Exceptions would be any poorly refractory, fine-grained clays that might react in the reducing zone behind the oxidized tip. Clay KO-3 is such an exception since laboratory tests show that the untempered briquettes badly spall at 800, 1000, 1200° C.

(Figure 9.9), the grog-tempered clay is weakened by bloating at 1200° C., and both completely melt away by 1400° C.

In another case, clay KK-3 was used to make smelting tuyeres during reconstructions of iron smelting in 1976 (Schmidt & Avery 1978). In those contexts, the tips melted away and the remaining sections became blocked up by iron slag. Clay BC-3, its substitution in 1978, survived all the smelts performed with significantly less melting and no blockage of the tip. The laboratory experiments show that tempered clay KK-3 bloats and melts by 1500° C. under oxidation. This reaction was initiated earlier, at 1400° C., under reduction.

Two factors probably contributed to the severe reactions of clay KK-3 during smelting. First, it is possible that reactions began behind the oxidized tip where a reducing atmosphere caused the high amount of iron oxides (10.5% by volume) to flux the clay at lower temperatures. Once the fluxing commenced and initiated melting, the surface of the tuyere wall would have been sealed off to the oxidizing atmosphere. These conditions would have permitted the original fluxing reactions to continue and become more severe with higher temperatures. Secondly, the relatively pure conditions of experimentation do not allow for a critical additional factor in the breakdown of clay KK-3. This factor is the effect of a basic slag wash, containing high amounts of FeO, MgO, or K_2O, on acidic tuyere surfaces which have a high silica content. The result is an additional fluxing reaction that chemically dissolves the affected clay (Shaw 1972). Besides being refractory, then, an ideal tuyere clay is one that is resistant to slag penetration.

Nonplastic Inclusions

The addition of broken sherd fragments to the tuyere and pottery clays clearly increases their structural stability (Tables 9.2 and 9.3).

They first act to minimize cracking during drying by opening up the paste for uniform drying. They then reduce the harmful effects of increasing temperature during smelting, firing, or use. The similar rates of thermal expansion for the paste and grog inclusions help reduce the chances of cracking or spalling from stresses created during heating (Rye 1976; 1981). This is illustrated in Figure 9.9 where extreme spalling or exploding occurred on the fine-grained, untempered briquettes of clay KO-3. The percentages of firing shrinkage are always the same or lower for the tempered briquettes than for the untempered ones. The percentages of apparent absorption and apparent porosity show that the tempered briquettes are usually more porous at elevated temperatures (1000, 1200° C.) than the untempered ones (Childs 1986:601–610). These various tests indicate that the voids created by the addition of grog act to minimize shrinking and to curtail cracking which can result as particular natural inclusions expand, such as quartz.

More significantly, the tempered briquettes are more refractory than their untempered counterparts particularly under oxidizing atmospheres. It is likely that the voids created by the added inclusions provide outlets for expanding gases that can cause bloating in the finer grained clays (Figure 9.8). They also create spaces that need to be filled before sintering can be completed and rapid melting can commence.

Resource Selection and Choice

The experiments described above show that the clays within each functional group (brick/termite mound and tuyere/pottery) vary in their reactions to the temperatures and atmospheres of iron smelting. As the outcome of these firing reactions influence the selection of suitable resources, means to predict how new clays might react to smelting conditions without having to conduct an entire smelt would be most beneficial. Various criteria for reliable predictions might evolve by initially comparing the fired reactions of different clays after a smelt with some of their physical characteristics in the raw state. Consistent correlations must then be found between particular fired and raw properties. Armed with physical markers of potential suitability during clay collection, iron workers can increase their ability to locate and gain access to a wider range of resources over the regional landscape.

A similar approach of collecting and testing many clay samples, along with interviewing modern informants about their criteria of selection, allows the archaeologist to assess the degree of choice available to and used by the ancient craftsmen. Such choice is important because it dictates the flexibility of a technology to expand or adapt. It also influences the susceptibility of a technology to external control over scarce or specialized materials by political, economic or other interest groups.

Among the brick and termite mound samples that could be used for furnace construction and smelting under reducing conditions, almost half show signs of high temperature problems at 1200° C., or of carbon spalling and disintegration at 600° C. and 800° C. Most of these damaged samples, but particularly the most reactive ones from termite mounds, contain considerable amounts of organics. It seems that slightly sandier, more porous materials with less organics respond better to reduction. In these cases, the small amounts of volatile carbon are released easily through the porous structure with the result that bloating is minimized (Hamer 1975:28). Since both the presence of organics and a sandy texture are visible to the naked eye, it should be possible, when choosing clays from above or below ground sources, to avoid organic-rich materials and select for relatively sandy ones.

Although the swamp clays, identified for tuyere making, might be more predictable and refractory as furnace construction materials, several factors discourage their use. First, the density and fine-grained nature of the tuyere clays, determined by briefly working the clay at the mining site, can lead to cracking, spalling and bloating. These potentially damaging effects must be alleviated by the addition of nonplastics. The labor and materials necessary to temper the quantity of clay required to build and line a furnace would have been costly and unnecessary. The natural porosity of the sandy brick and termite mound clays actually provides all the desireable characteristics to minimize cracking and thermal stresses.

Secondly, several physical characteristics of the modern swamp clays match those of the ancient tuyere sherds (Childs 1986) thereby identifying the general clay source of the prehistoric tuyere makers. Potential swamps were usually located at some distance from the Early Iron Age smelting sites (Schmidt 1982). Transporting the hundreds of pounds of material required to build a furnace would be unnecessary when convenient termite mounds or clayey soils were more readily available at a smelting site. In particular, the quantity and accessibility of aboveground termite mounds or the sandy clays underlying the smelting sites may have made either materials more desireable than the more refractory, but less accessible clays from swamps. Their suboptimal thermal properties, as we have seen, may be accomodated by making thick bricks and thickly lining the furnace pit.

The natural characteristics of the readily available termite mounds, the sandier, upper layers of clays bordering the swamps, and the clayey soils on the ridge tips and flanks means that a wide variety of suitable resources were available to build a furnace. The adjustments made to minimize chances of debilitating structural damage during smelting, in combination with some degree of selectivity for sandy, organic-free materials, insures that other sources of materials such as the swamps are totally unnecessary and are quite inappropriate.

The fact that tuyeres are used to create the highest temperatures in the furnace and therefore become subjected to the heat produced, underscores their specialized function and physical requirements. Although critical, physical testing of all the samples from the Kagera region shows that refractoriness is not the only criterion upon which to define an optimal tuyere clay. Based on their refractory properties, a few of the brick samples could be used for tuyere construction. The primary reason for the poor suitability of these brick clays is their lack of plastic forming qualities. The high sand content in these materials limits their ability to be shaped into thin-walled, tubular forms.

All of the identified tuyere and pottery clays had to be fine-grained and plastic in order to be selected. But beyond these criteria, the evidence suggests that optimal tuyere clays for smelting are actually very difficult to identify. This is because it is almost impossible to determine their refractory quality without subjecting them to a smelt. The wide variety of responses by the tuyere and pottery samples to the laboratory firing conditions emphasizes the care necessary to select suitable clays for tuyere making. It also indicates the limited availability of optimal clays and the existance of a functional hierarchy of swamp resources.

Among the tested samples, the least functional one (KO-3) cannot be used for smelting and probably not for forging since it spalls by explosion and melts by 1400° C. under oxidation. The tuyere clay (KK-3) that was used for lower temperature forging severely bloats by 1500° C., in the middle range of the blast zone temperatures commonly found during a smelt. Tuyere clays BC-3, L-3, and KY-3 become more refractory and useable for smelting when nonplastics are added to the paste (Figure 9.8). Two pottery clays (L-4 and KY-4) collected in higher layers of the swamps, on the other hand, do not benefit as much from grog tempering. Lastly, several isolated areas in large swamps yielded the best clays (RW-3, R-3 and B-4) for iron smelting.

These differences in performance and suitability are mostly due to chemical impurities derived from very localized variation in clay formation (Childs 1986). Such differences can exist between nearby fingers of land which separate off individual areas of the same swamp. Nearby clays can have somewhat different chemical make-ups because the parent rocks on the ridges above the swamp borders can vary somewhat and can weather under differing conditions. Therefore, grittiness and plasticity can be used to discover the best potential clay in a swamp for smelting tuyeres and the addition of grog temper might enhance its performance, but careful selection can be quickly undermined when the ultimate test, an actual smelt, is performed.

Such difficulties in clay selection are lessened for lower temperature operations such as forging and pottery making. These technologies have less specialized needs for combatting heat and atmosphere. Since they have similar requirements for a fine-grained texture and plasticity, however, the swamps provide an almost endless source of acceptable materials. The addition of grog should enhance their performances even more.

Conclusions

The atmospheric and thermal conditions found during iron smelting requires that clay resources used for various aspects of the technological process have specific physical properties. This paper demonstrated that testing and understanding the firing properties of modern refractories, along with their accessibility over the Kagera region, is vital to establishing the criteria of resource selection used today and in prehistory. An idea of the range of physical and thermal variation among the local clays is important to understanding compromises the iron workers might make between technological control, labor efficiency, and accessibility to materials.

When the prehistoric artifacts were compared to the fired clay briquettes, using the same tests and methods, some of the selection criteria and choices used in prehistory could be suggested. Clearly, however, these examinations focused on the inherent properties of the materials and the technological decisions made to manipulate specific properties. The final task, for another paper, must be to determine if and how cultural factors, such as outside control over specific resource locations, influenced resource selection choices and iron production in general during the Early Iron Age.

Notes

1. The sample numbers refer to the collection site in the letter prefix (see Figure 9.5) and the clay functional group in the number suffix. All brick clays are assigned 1, all termite mound samples are 2, the tuyere clays are 3, and the pottery clays are 4.

References Cited

Arnold, D. "Ethnomineralogy of Ticul, Yucatan potters: Etics and emics." *American Antiquity.* 36:20–40, 1971.

_____. "Some Principles for Paste Analyses and Interpretation: A Preliminary Formulation." *Journal of the Steward Anthropological Soc.* 6(1):33–47, 1975.

Avery, D. and Schmidt, P. "A Metallurgical Study of the Iron Bloomery, Particularly as Practiced in Buhaya." *Journal of Metals.* Oct.:14–20, 1979.

Childs, S.T. "Style in Technology: A View of the Early Iron Age Iron Smelting Technology through its Refractory Ceramics." Unpublished Ph.D. thesis, Boston University, 1986.

Childs, S.T. and Schmidt, P. "Experimental Iron Smelting—The Genesis of a Hypothesis with Implications for African Prehistory." in *African Iron Technology,* R. Haaland & P. Shinnie (eds.). Univ. of Oslo Press, 1985.

Clews, F., Ball, F., and Green, A.T. "The Action of Carbon Monoxide on Refractory Materials: Some Aspects of the Catalytic Action of Ferruginous Glass of Iron Spots." *Trans. British Ceramic Soc.* 45(7):251–255, 1946.

Cline, W. *Mining and Metallurgy in Negro Africa.* General series of Anthropology. Wisconsin, 1937.

Furnas, C. "Kinetics of Some Reactions of Interest to Ceramists: The Disintegration of Blast-furnace Linings due to Carbon Deposition." *Journal American Ceramic Soc.* 19(6):177–186, 1936.

Hamer, F. *The Potter's Dictionary of Materials and Techniques.* London: Pitman Pub, 1975.

Hesse, P. "A Chemical and Physical Study of the Soils of Termite Mounds in East Africa." *Journal of Ecology.* 43(2):449–461, 1955.

Matson, F. "A Study of Temperatures used in Firing Ancient Mesopotamian Pottery." in *Science and Archaeology,* R. Brill (ed.). Cambridge: MIT Press, 1971.

Rice, P. "Ceramic Continuity and Change in the Valley of Guatemala: A Technological Analysis." in *The Ceramics of Kaminaljuyu,* R. Wetherington (ed.). Penn. State Press, 1978.

Rigby, G., Booth, H., and Green, A.T. "Disintegration of Fire Clay Products by Mixtures of CO and CO2." *Trans. British Ceramic Soc.* 43(4):73–80, 1944.

Rye, O. "Keeping your Temper under Control: Materials and the Manufacture of Papuan Pottery." *Archaeology and Physical Anthropology in Oceania.* 11(2):106–137, 1976.

———. *Pottery Technology.* Washington: Taraxacum, 1981.

Schmidt, P. "Early Iron Age Settlements and Industrial Locales in Westlake." Tanzania Notes and Records 84/85:77–94, 1982.

Schmidt, P. and Avery, D. "Complex Iron Smelting and Prehistoric Culture in Tanzania." *Science.* 201:1085–1089, 1978.

Schmidt, P. and Childs, S.T. "Innovation and Industry During the Early Iron Age in East Africa: The KM2 and KM3 sites of NW Tanzania." *African Archaeological Review* 3:53–94, 1985.

Shaw, K. *Refractories and Their Uses.* New York: Wiley & Sons, 1972.

Shepard, A.O. *Ceramics for the Archaeologist.* Carnegie Institute of Washington. Public. #609, 1965.

Tylecote, R. *A History of Metallurgy.* London: The Metals Society, 1976.

Tylecote, R., Austin, J., and Wraith, A. "The Mechanism of the Bloomery Process in Shaft Furnaces." *J. of the Iron and Steel Institute.* 209:342–363, 1971.

Figure 9.1 Map of the Kagera region in Tanzania, East Africa. The cross-hatching delimits the area of clay collection in Figure 9.5.

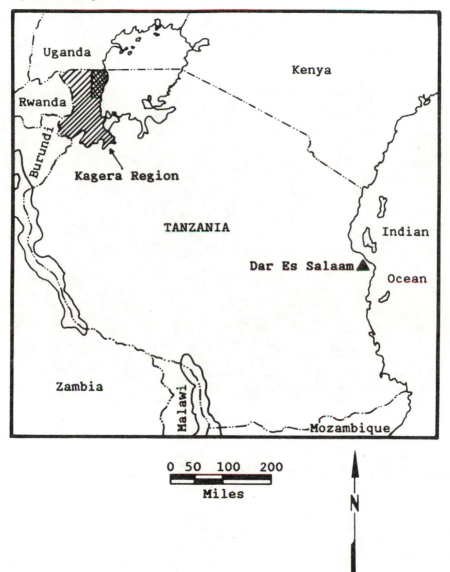

154

Figure 9.2 The profile of a brick fragment as it once lay on a furnace structure. The hardened surface near the scale faced the smelting activity, the opposite weathered surface was next to the furnace exterior that was minimally heated, and the smoothed side had other bricks on top of it.

Figure 9.3 An excavated furnace with some of the liner in situ from the KM-2 site in the Kagera region (Schmidt and Childs 1985). The furnace diameter is approximately one meter.

156

Figure 9.4 An excavated tuyere section from the KM-3 site. The tip is vitrified and slagged, behind which the clay is oxidized. The end of the section is reduced, while the interior surface of the pipe is oxidized.

Figure 9.5 The locations of the collected clay samples. The coastal topographical zone is at the lake edge, the white areas constitute the ridge-flank zone, and the remaining areas are swamplands.

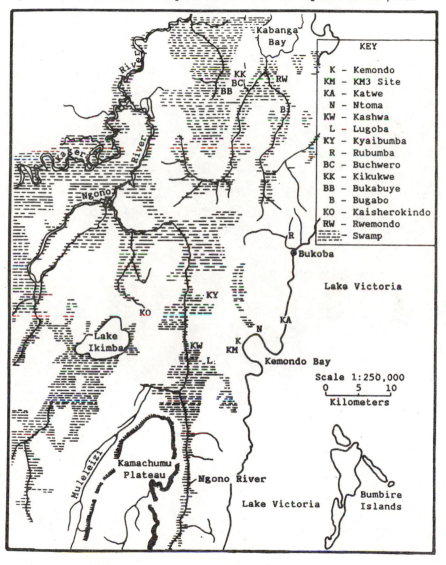

KEY

K	–	Kemondo
KM	–	KM3 Site
KA	–	Katwe
N	–	Ntoma
KW	–	Kashwa
L	–	Lugoba
KY	–	Kyaibumba
R	–	Rubumba
BC	–	Buchwero
KK	–	Kikukwe
BB	–	Bukabuye
B	–	Bugabo
KO	–	Kaisherokindo
RW	–	Rwemondo
≡≡≡	–	Swamp

Scale 1:250,000

0   5   10

Kilometers

Figure 9.6 An interior piece of a termite mound with many passageways.

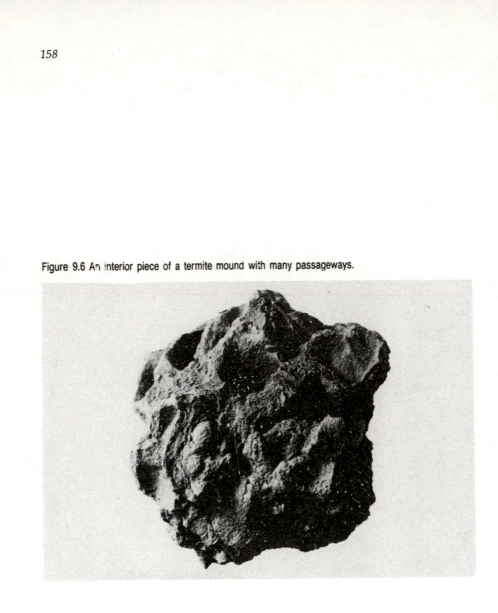

Table 9.1
Reactions of the Brick and Termite Mound Clay Samples to Thermal and Atmospheric Conditions

		Temperatures (°C)					
Clay ID	*Atmos.*	*600*	*800*	*1000*	*1200*	*1400*	*1500*
Brick samples							
K-1	OX	—				B	B
	RE					IM/IB	IM/IB
N-1	OX	—				IB	BM
	RE	CS			IM	B/M	B/M
BC-1	OX	—					B
	RE						B
R-1	OX	—					
	RE	CS	CS				IB
L-1	OX	—					
	RE					IM	IM/B
Termite mound samples							
KA-2	OX	—					IB
	RE	CS	CSD		IB/IM	M	M
KM-2	OX	—				B	B
	RE	CS	CS		B	B	B
BB-2	OX	—					IB
	RE					M	M/B
RW-2	OX	—				B	M
	RE	CSD	CSD		B	B	IM/B

Key: OX = Oxidizing atmosphere; RE = Reducing atmosphere; — = No data; CS = Carbon spalling; CSD = Carbon spalling and disintegration; IM = Initial melting; M = Melting; IB = Initial bloating; B = Bloating.

Table 9.2

Thermal Reactions of the Untempered and Tempered Tuyere and Pottery Clay Samples in a Reducing Atmosphere

Clay ID	Temper	Temperatures (°C)					
		600	800	1000	1200	1400	1500
Tuyere samples							
KK-3	UN	CS				IB/IM	B/M
	T	CS				IB/IM	B/M
BC-3	UN	CS	CS		IM	IM	IB/IM
	T	CS	CS			IB/IM	IB/IM
KW-3	UN				IB	B	B
	T				IB	IB	IB
R-3	UN					IM	IM
	T					IM	IM
RW-3	UN						IB
	T	CS					IB
L-3	UN						IB
	T						IB
KY-3	UN						B/IM
	T						B/IM
KO-3	UN		S	S	S	M	
	T				IB	M	
Pottery samples							
B-4	UN						B
	T						
L-4	T						B
KY-4	T						B

Key: UN = Untempered; T = Tempered; CS = Carbon spalling; IM = Initial melting; M = Melting; IB = Initial bloating; B = Bloating; S = Spalling.

Table 9.3
Thermal Reactions of the Untempered and Tempered Tuyere and Pottery Clay Samples in an Oxidizing Atmosphere

		Temperatures (°C)				
Clay ID	Temper	800	1000	1200	1400	1500
Tuyere samples						
KK-3	UN					B/M
	T					B/M
BC-3	UN					B
	T					
KW-3	UN					I/B
	T					I/B
R-3	UN					
	T					
RW-3	UN					
	T					
L-3	UN					B
	T					
KY-3	UN					B
	T					
KO-3	UN				E/M	
	T				E/M	
Pottery samples						
B-4	UN					
	T					
L-4	T					B
KY-4	T					B

Key: UN = Untempered; T = Tempered; IB = Initial bloating; B = Bloating; M = Melting; E = Exploded.

Figure 9.7 A briquette of clay RW-2 fired at 600° C. in a reducing atmosphere. The carbon deposits grew under the clay surface and caused extensive cracking and spalling. The briquette was approximately one inch square before it completely disintegrated.

Figure 9.8 Cross-sections of untempered and grog-tempered briquettes made of clay KY-3. The two briquettes at the left were fired to 1400° C., and the two at the right were fired to 1500° C., all under oxidation. The untempered briquette fired to 1500° C. has bloated.

Figure 9.9 The briquettes of clay KO-3 fired under reduction. The ones in the top row are untempered and the ones in the bottom row are grog tempered. The original briquettes were cut in half when possible: The left piece is the surface view and the right piece provides a cross-sectional view.

600°C   800°C   1000°C   1200°C

PART FOUR

Ceramic Analysis and the Study of Formation Processes

10

A Materials Science Perspective on Hunter-Gatherer Pottery

Kenneth C. Reid

Center for Northwest Anthropology,
Washington State University

The thesis of this paper is that the archaeological record of hunter gatherer pottery is best understood not as an accumulation of increasingly well documented artifactual evidence, but as the expression of a constant relation between prehistoric cooking needs and subsequent weathering processes. The observations that prompt the hypothesis come from ethnographic accounts of native cooking pots in northwestern North America, discussed here in terms of their performance and preservation properties. The research is part of an ongoing inquiry into the correspondence between the archaeological appearance of ceramics and the behavioral use of cooking pots in prehistory (Reid 1984a,1984b).

Cooking needs are understood as the temperatures required to produce palatable effects. Temperature needs are an expression of the relation between cooking heats on the one hand and the firing temperatures of cooking pots on the other. Weathering processes include the mechanical and chemical breakdown over time of potsherds on or in the ground. Holding other things constant, these processes are expected to vary inversely with latitude: mechanical weathering, principally frost action, is the primary agency of sherd destruction to the north, while to the south chemical disintegration of sherds occurs in areas of locally high precipitation. Our concern here will be with mechanical weathering as the taphonomic filter through which the pots of northern hunters must pass. In developing the argument we will pursue three lines of inquiry.

Acknowledgments: I thank Allan H. Smith, emeritus professor of anthropology at Washington State University, for helpful comments on an earlier version.

The first concerns the temperatures and kinds of heat needed to cook the foods in question. Here the definitions and classification of cooking processes provided by modern food science and nutritional research are essential. Next, we want to discover how ethnographic pots might function as cooking tools. We will do this by looking at accounts of their production and use from a materials science perspective (Bronitsky 1986). Finally, we must ask how the archaeological distribution of potsherds fits the functional solutions to the cooking problems that we have isolated. At this point, a taphonomic approach coupled with controlled laboratory experiment is most helpful.

Cooking Process

Hunting and gathering is the oldest human subsistence pattern, and pottery everywhere made its first appearance within the context of food remains reflecting this adaptation. It is, therefore, helpful to look at how hunted and gathered foods are prepared before asking how cooking pots work. Because the archaeological vocabulary of food preparation retains several misnomers such as "earth oven" and "stone boiling" (Tylor 1964) that tend to confuse analysis, the following discussion of the cooking process employs the thermal and moisture definitions of modern food science research (Lundberg and Kotschevar 1965) to avoid these difficulties.

The principal foods cooked by hunters and gatherers include the meat of game animals and birds, fish and shellfish, and seeds, nuts, berries and roots. The actual combination of foods taken in any given case depends on environment, but the nutritional value and caloric accessibility of their protein, fat, and carbohydrate fractions are usually increased by controlled heating. The cooking methods commonly used by hunter-gatherers fall into dry heating and moist heating categories. The former includes broiling, roasting, baking, and parching; the latter, simmering, boiling, and steaming (Table 10.1). Dry cooking temperatures vary from about 150° C., the range at which meat begins to broil or roast, to the red heat (550–625° C.) of coals and embers used in parching seeds. The heats involved in moist cooking are significantly lower, starting at about 85° C. when simmering begins, and continuing past the boiling threshold at 100° C. to the superheated (100° C.+) temperatures achieved by pressure cooking with steam.

The ethnography of hunting shows that when game and fish are fat and abundant, the meat is often cooked directly over radiant heat (broiled) or in an oven surrounded by heated air (roasted). Broiling is a simple, quick, open flame technique that brings the meat to an internal temperature of 60–80° C., while roasting requires more time and an oven for the convectional circulation of hot dry air. By comparison with moist cooking alternatives, both broiling and roasting are relatively unthrifty methods that fail to access much of the animal's food value, especially marrow fat or "bone grease" and blood.

The other dry cooking techniques of parching and baking refer to the milling of seeds and nuts and their processing as flour. Parching involves exposing the seeds directly to very high temperatures, usually glowing coals, in order to burst their starchy kernels. The popped seeds can then be eaten directly, stored, or milled for flour. Baking describes the cooking of flour and water mixtures (not meat or vegetables) in contained dry heat at roasting temperatures (Lundberg and Kotschevar 1965:89).

Moist cooking methods occur at lower and more controlled temperatures than broiling or roasting, and involve the convectional heating of food with currents of water or steam instead of dry air. There are three basic ways to do this. Steaming cooks food under greater than atmospheric pressure with currents of contained moist air, usually in pressure cooking pits ("earth ovens") with the food placed between alternating layers of preheated rocks and moist vegetation. When the pit is capped, the food cooks under pressure of the seal. Pressure cooking with steam is particularly well suited for cooking large starchy plants such as roots and tubers because the high temperatures (100° C. depending on pressure) successfully gelatinize the carbohydrates, and the finished product can usually be pressed into a more compact form for storage or transport.

The other moist cooking techniques of simmering and boiling both require a watertight container that is capable of holding liquid food long enough for cooking to occur. Food is added to water which is kept heated either by adding hot rocks to the contents or by directly exposing the vessel wall to radiant heat. Simmering occurs when the water is heated to between 85–88° C. and bubbles form below the surface, without breaking at the surface (Lundberg and Kotschevar 1965:33). Boiling occurs at about 100° C. when the bubbles break at and roil the surface. Simmering temperatures are ideal for the stewing or souping of meat, and for the rendering of oils from nonstarchy seeds and nuts, or bone grease from smashed bone fragments. Moist cooking of meat at a simmer reduces the white connective tissue or collagen to a gel, but cooking it at a boil coagulates the protein, resulting in toughness and shrinkage (Lundberg and Kotshcevar 1965:5,83, 115). In addition, boiling is inefficient for rendering of bone grease or nut oil because the roiled surface prevents skimming of released oils and fat (Leechman 1951:355–356). However, where boiling does become adaptive is in the cooking of starchy seeds (Braun 1983:116–117). Starch from cereal grains and roots begins to thicken between about 62–72° C., but does not completely gelatinize until 93° C. (Lundberg and Kotschevar 1965:6). The thorough reduction of a starchy seed mass to a digestible gel, therefore, requires high and sustained cooking heats that approximate steaming rather than simmering temperatures.

This simple classification of cooking modes leads to the following predictions. First, and most obviously, the modest volume capacity of cookpots by comparison with steaming pits suggests that they will be selected against where bulky root crops are a food staple. Pressure cooking pits are the most energetically efficient way to process quantities of bulky plants, while the more particulate cereal grains are probably most efficiently gelatinized by pot boiling. A broadly covariant relationship should, therefore, exist between the exploitation of carbohydrate seeds and starchpots built for boiling.

A second expectation is that in situations where game is the major staple, we should see widespread use of cookpots for stewing and souping meat, and especially for rendering bone grease, often a critically important winter food among northern hunters (Denig 1930:509, 584; Speth and Spielmann 1983). The remainder of this analysis will attempt to piece together a general descriptive account of northern meatpots and greasepots from the scattered ethnographic reports, concentrating on performance and preservation properties rather than surface decoration or motor habits of the potters. For the time being, the ethnographic data are accepted at face value. However, it should be apparent that much of this testimony needs additional experimental support before it can be fully accepted as archaeologically relevent.

Northern Meatpot in the Nineteenth Century

Ethnographic mention of clay cooking pots in northwestern North America occurs frequently but usually with little accompanying detail. For example, the Gros Ventre, Assiniboine, Plains Cree, Northern Saltaux, Kaska, Kutchin, Tanana, and Tainana are all reported to have cooked in pots, but in none of the accounts are clay vessels described in any detail. However, fairly specific first hand ethnographic and "memory technology" descriptions are available for some groups. These include the three divisions of the Blackfoot (Ewers 1945), the Kutenai (Ray 1942:136–137; Schaeffer 1952; Smith 1984:221), and the Sarsi (Sapir 1923) on the northwestern plains; the Ingalik (Osgood 1940:146–148) and Koyukon (de Laguna 1947:142–148) of the western subarctic; and a continuous zone of arctic Eskimo groups ranging from the Mackenzie delta on the east to peninsular Siberia on the west (Stefansson 1914:312; Spencer 1959:470–474; Nelson 1899:201–202; Bogoras 1904:186).

A general ware description of these northern pots can be abstracted from the traits of manufacture and use listed in Table 10.2. Features that recur over an extraordinarily wide geographic area include the use of blood, "glue" (probably sturgeon blood), or sea mammal oil in the raw paste; use of organic fibers such as animal hair, feathers, grass and sedge stems, and even twigs to brace the vessel walls while drying; and the inclusion of sand, grit, crushed limestone, and other minerals as temper. The completed vessel was flat bottomed and bucket shaped with straight or flaring walls in all examples except the North Alaskan Eskimo, who produced a conoidal form. The pots were thick walled (10 cm is typical) with even thicker bottoms. Wide diameter orifices were the rule, with the opening often as wide as the pot was tall. Bail holes to accommodate handles made of bison neck gristle, withe, or bone are reported by Blood, Tobacco Plains Kutenai, and Sarsi informants. Ewers (1945:296) interprets this trait among the Blackfoot in terms of suspension from a tripod over a hearth, while Kutenai and Sarsi informants report they were installed so pots could be carried about—Jack and Jill fashion—while on the move.

The vessels are commonly described as dried in the sun or beside a hearth, or "baked" rather than fired to a red heat ca. 550–625° C. The various mentions of drying, heat hardening, and baking suggest that they were exposed to subceramic heating thresholds sufficient to drive out the water in the clay body, but usually not high enough to decompose organic inclusions, still less achieve a ceramic fabric (Figure 10.1). For example, small fires of shavings were set inside Ingalik pots to burn off protruding edges of the feathers added to the paste, indicating that "baking" occurred at temperatures below the range of organic decomposition. True firing may have been practiced by the North Alaskan Eskimo who exposed the finished pot to oil fed flames, but still only produced "poorly fired" results. Vessels were commonly oiled or greased inside and out before and after each use, and the interiors were occasionally lined with animal skin or membrane to further waterproof them.

The pots were used for cooking meat or fish, or rendering oils or fat from bone fragments or blubber. There is no evidence that carbohydrate seeds or tubers were cooked in them. However, the specific method of cooking is described in only six instances. The Tobacco Plains Kutenai and North Alaskan Eskimo used pots for hot stone cooking ("stone boiling"), while the Ingalik cooked by placing the vessel beside, but not in or over the flames and the Koyukon, by nesting it in embers rather than over flames. This would imply exposure to temperatures of less than about 625° C. Only the pit-"baked" variants of the St. Mary's Kutenai and the Blackfoot are said to have been usable over open flames.

Greased Blackfoot pots are reported to have become hardened by repeated use, again implying a low initial firing temperature.

In five instances the vessels are described as fragile and easily broken, and the Ingalik and Mackenzie Eskimo pots were vulnerable to disintegration after prolonged exposure to dampness. Nevertheless, they were valued possessions and considered completely portable, suggesting that the link between sedentism and pottery has been overstated. Probably any tool that is useful enough to keep and small enough for carriage is compatible with residentially mobile adaptations:

Ingalik
- "If they are to be carried from one village to another, they are packed in a birch bark basket with grass tightly around them on the outside and the inside also filled up tightly with grass" (Osgood 1940:148).

Koyukon
- ". . . pots were easily broken and so were always carried in cases of skin" (de Laguna 1947:141).

Kutenai
- "Traditions have come down of the hunting party making its way on snowshoes through the mountain passes, men and women carrying the heavier camp equipment while one of the smaller children carried the family cooking pot" (Schaeffer 1952:3).
- "By means of . . . bail, the vessel could be suspended from a person's back by a thong while traveling" (Schaeffer 1952:4).

Sarsi
- ". . . in the earlier days the clay vessels were carried by their handles of withes or bone by the women and children, who walked by the side of the dog travois" (Sapir 1923:248-249).

Piegan
- "It had two holes near the rim for a handle. When she moved camp she carried it in a laced rawhide container which was packed on the top of a packhorse's load" (Ewers 1945:295).

Finally, many of the accounts provide specific, named locations for the sources of the clays used, often in contexts indicating that these were the best clays available. However, alertness to superior materials does not necessarily imply reliance on them. Sapir's informant explained that "emergency pots" could be made from available clays (1923:251), a hint that for northern hunters the vessels functioned as more than a situational convenience.

Performance Properties

Primitive pottery is usually classified as terra cotta or earthenware on the basis of its typically low firing temperature and high porosity (Rice 1987:5). Terra cottas are ceramic fabrics fired to a range high enough for sintering of clay particles to begin, a process that typically starts at about 350° C. and is completed by 700° C. (Hamer 1975:122). Earthenwares are fired at temperatures high enough for vitrification to begin, when the clay particles fuse together as glass. This begins to occur between 800–900° C. and is completed at about 1200° C. (Figure 1.1).

Clay pots fired to sintering or vitrification thresholds are true ceramics, capable of holding liquids indefinitely and conducting heat from one surface to the other without cracking. Their resistance to failure from repeated heating and cooling is due primarily to their relatively high porosity. This allows them to expand and contract without wall failure because the pore spaces tend to arrest and absorb the energy of propagating cracks (Cardew 1969:77). The more completely vitrified such a pot becomes, the more effective it is at conducting heat, especially if higher firings are accompanied by thinner walls and a more spherical shape (Braun 1983). In addition, hotter and longer firings harden the surface, making it more resistant to crack initiation. However, the greater brittleness resulting from fabric homogeneity can mean that once a crack starts, it will travel further, often lending to vessel failure (Rice 1987:368).

In terms of performance properties, a clay vessel used for hot stone cooking has quite different design requirements than a boiling pot. The basic problem for the hot stone cook is to keep the heat in the vessel, not to transmit the heat through the pot from exterior to interior. The analogy with hot stone cooking containers is to a thermos rather than a kettle; the engineering principle is one of insulation rather than conduction. Design characteristics should include a thick, porous fabric that will retain rather than conduct heat, a watertight interior, an overthickened, flat, stable base that can absorb the radiant heat and impact energy of the hot stones, and straight or flaring walls with a wide mouth to facilitate skimming or rendering of bone grease. Since boiling is not the objective, constricted orifices to inhibit evaporation are not predicted. Finally, very low firing temperatures make sense because low fired or unfired clays are better insulators than conductors of heat. As first the pore water, and then the bound water, is driven out of clay bodies by prolonged drying, heat hardening, or baking, and as organic inclusions decompose, the amount of pore space increases until sintering begins, after which the size and number of pores begins to decrease (Rice 1987:94). In other words, unfired subceramic and underfired terra cotta vessels have relatively high insulation but low conduction properties, making them better suited for hot stone cooking than open fire cooking.

Another potential advantage of subceramics and low fired terra cottas is their position along the continuous variable of "fragility." Fragility can be understood in terms of either resistance to crack initiation or resistance to crack propagation, but not both simultaneously (Rice 1987:362–363). Thus, for pots that are not moved around much but that are exposed to random impacts from people and household animals, hard surfaced pots with high resistance to crack initiation make sense. However, for mobile hunters who pack everything with them, shock absorbing pots that resist crack propagation are potentially more efficient.

Preservation Properties

The absence of archaeological evidence for the subceramic pots described to ethnographers by informants, but not actually seen by them has always been the main argument against native testimony of their former use (Ewers 1945:295). A taphonomic perspective on the problem has been conspicuously lacking, though it has been suggested that archaeological remains of unfired pots might survive in caves or rockshelters offering protection from rainfall (Griffin 1965:295). However, the northern distribution of these vessels argues instead for mechanical breakdown through frost action as the major cause of sherd disintegration. How this might occur has been investigated experimentally with respect to clay bodies fired in the terra cotta and earthenware range (Skibo, Schiffer, and Reid 1988).

An experiment was set up to explore the hypothesis that the high apparent porosity of fiber-tempered pottery made it especially susceptible to mechanical destruction from the seasonal freezing and thawing of absorbed pore water over long periods of time (Reid 1984). The procedure involved firing groups of untempered, organically tempered, and sand tempered briquettes to temperatures ranging from 550–950° C. at 100° C. intervals, then submitting each group to between five and ten freeze-thaw cycles within a water saturated sand matrix contained by an environmental chamber. Results showed that none of the briquettes fired at 550° C., regardless of temper type, could survive five freeze-thaw cycles without breaking. However, all of the briquettes fired at 950° C., again regardless of temper, survived ten freeze-thaw cycles without breaking. Among specimens fired at the 650° C., 750° C., and 850° C.

intervals, breakage patterns varied considerably according to the temper category and number of freeze-thaw cycles to which they were subjected (Skibo, Schiffer, and Reid 1988).

Results of the experiment support the idea that sherd durability is determined less by apparent than by total porosity (Rice 1987:351). Thus, the high apparent porosity of high fired organically tempered specimens with numerous open pores at the surface did not influence their durability at up to ten freeze-thaw cycles, while the high total porosity of the low fired specimens resulted in their breakdown within five freeze-thaw cycles, regardless of how they were tempered. The prediction for the hunter-gatherer subceramic meatpots described earlier, which were typically fired well below the lower experimental threshold of 550° C., would be virtually zero survival in cold seasonal environments. High porosity improves insulation value for hot stone cooking and perhaps shock absorbing capability as well, but the performance properties of the pot are related more or less inversely to the preservation properties of the potsherd.

In northwestern North America within the past two hundred years several groups of residentially mobile hunter-gatherers made subceramic clay pots to stew meat and render fat and oil. A materials science perspective on their manufacture and use suggests that the pots functioned as a kind of primitive thermos, the underfired clay acting to insulate the contents after they were brought to a simmer with hot stones. The pattern of their use across the northern plains and western subarctic and arctic suggests a common response to comparable physiological "calorie/rehydration" requirements. Regular intakes of fats and warm fluids are an adaptive requirement for winter mobility in cold seasonal environments (Steegman, Hurlich, and Winterhalder 1983:328–329; Speth and Spielmann 1983). Experimental simulations of the effects of frost action on low fired briquettes suggest that subceramic meatpots are not much more archaeologically durable over time than birch bark containers, but they were certainly more efficient cooking tools (Hearne 1911:305–306; Honigmann 1946:54; Mason 1946:19; Schaeffer 1952:2–3), and perhaps as fully portable.

Finally, the distribution of northern pottery in the past was presumably more continuous than the scattered native testimony itself. Certainly the surviving accounts override rather than coincide with the major ethnic and linguistic divisions represented by the sample. Perhaps it is appropriate to conclude with the suggestion that subceramic meatpots represent the technical precedents for more archaeologically durable ceramic boiling pots, the latter appearing when circumstances such as resource intensification made them locally useful.

References Cited

Bogoras, Waldemar. *The Chukchee. The Jesup Pacific Expedition.* Memoirs of the American Museum of Natural History, Vol 7, Part 1. New York, 1904.

Braun, David P. "Pots as Tools." in *Archaeological Hammers and Theories,* edited by James A. Moore and Arthur S. Keene, pp. 127–134. Academic Press, New York, 1983.

Bronitsky, Gordon. "The Use of Materials Science Techniques in the Study of Pottery Construction and Use." *Advances in Archaeological Method and Theory.* 9:209–276, 1986.

Cardew, Michael. *Pioneer Pottery.* St. Martin's Press, New York, 1969.

Denig, Edwin T. "Indian Tribes of the Upper Missouri," edited with notes and biographical sketch by J.N.B. Hewitt. *Bureau of American Ethnology Annual Report.* 46:375–628. Washington, D.C., 1930.

Ewers, John C. "The Case for Blackfoot Pottery." *American Anthropologist.* 47:289–299, 1945.

Griffin, James B. "Appendix: Prehistoric Pottery from Southeastern Alberta." in *Introduction to the Archaeology of Alberta, Canada,* by H.M. Wormington and Richard G. Forbis, pp. 209–248. Denver Museum of Natural History Proceedings No. 11, 1965.

Hamer, Frank. *The Potter's Dictionary of Materials and Techniques.* Watson-Guptill Publications, New York, 1975.

de Laguna, Frederica. "The Prehistory of Northern America as Seen from the Yukon." *Memoirs of the Society for American Archaeology.* 12(3), Part 2, 1947.

Leechman, Douglas. "Bone Grease." *American Antiquity.* 16:355–356, 1951.

Lundberg, Donald E., and Kotschevar, Lendal H. *Understanding Cooking.* The University Store, University of Massachusetts, Amherst, 1965.

Nelson, Edward W. *The Eskimo about Bering Strait.* Bureau of American Ethnology Annual Report 18, Washington, D.C., 1899.

Osgood, Cornelius. *Ingalik Material Culture.* Yale University Publications in Anthropology 22, New Haven, 1940.

Ray, Verne F. "Culture Element Distributions: XXII." Plateau. *Anthropological Records.* 8(2):98–262, 1942.

Reid, Kenneth C. "Fire and Ice: New Evidence for the Production and Preservation of Fiber-Tempered Pottery in the Mid-Latitude Lowlands," *American Antiquity.* 49:55–76, 1984.

Rice, Prudence M. *Pottery Analysis.* University of Chicago Press, Chicago, 1987.

Sapir, Edward. "A Note on Sarcee Pottery." *American Anthropologist.* 25:247–253, 1923.

Schaeffer, Claude E. *Molded Pottery Among the Kutenai Indians.* Montana State University Anthropology and Sociology Papers 6, Missoula, 1952.

Skibo, James M., Schiffer, Michael B., and Reid, Kenneth C. "Organic Tempered Pottery: An Experimental Study." *American Antiquity.* (in press), 1988.

Smith, Allan H. *Kutenai Indian Subsistence and Settlement Patterns, Northwest Montana.* Center for Northwest Anthropology Project Report No. 2, Vol. 2, Washington State University, Pullman, 1984.

Spencer, Robert F. *The North Alaskan Eskimo.* Bureau of American Ethnology Bulletin 171, Washington, DC., 1959.

Speth, John D., and Spielmann, Katherine A. "Energy Source, Protein Metabolism, and Hunter-Gatherer Subsistence Strategies." *Journal of Anthropological Archaeology.* 2:1–31, 1983.

Steegman, A. Theodore, Jr., Hurlich, Marshall G., and Winterhalder, Bruce. "Coping with Cold and Other Challenges of the Boreal Forest: An Overview." in *Boreal Forest Adaptations: The Northern Algonkians,* edited by A. Theodore Steegman, Jr., pp. 317–351. Plenum Press, New York, 1983.

Stefánsson, Vihjlámur. *The Stefansson-Anderson Arctic Expedition of the American Museum.* Preliminary Ethnological Report. Anthropological Papers of the American Museum of Natural History 14, New York, 1914.

Tylor, Edward B. "Appendix: Fire, Cooking, and Vessels." in *Research into the Early History of Mankind,* edited and abridged from the 3rd revised edition (1878) by Paul Bohannon. University of Chicago Press, pp. 243–290, 1964.

Table 10.1

Classification of Dry and Moist Cooking Methods Commonly Used by Hunter-Gatherers

Temperature (°C)	Heat Mode	
	Dry	*Moist*
85–88		Simmering, stewing, rendering
100		Boiling
100+		Steaming
150–200	Broiling	
150–250	Roasting, baking	
550–625	Parching	

Source: Data from Lundberg and Kotschevar 1965.

Table 10.2
Manufacture and Use Date for Subceramic Cooking Pots in Northwestern North America

	Blackfoot	Piegan	Blood	Tobacco Plains Kutenai	St. Mary's Kutenai	Sarsi	Ingalik	Koyukon	West Alaskan Eskimo	North Alaskan Eskimo	Mackenzie Eskimo	Siberian Eskimo (Yuit)
Manufacture												
Blood/"glue"/oil				+	+					+		+
Organic fiber		+	+			+	+	+	+	+	+	
Mineral temper				+	+	+	+	+	+	+	+	+
Dried only	+	+	+	+		?		+			+	
"Baked" only					+	?	+		+	?		
Fired to red heat										?		
Oiled, greased or lined		+	+				+	+	+			
Flat bottomed		+	+	+	+	+	+	+				+
Conoidal				+		+				+		
Bail holes			+									

	I	II	III	IV	V	VI	VII	VIII	IX	X	XI	XII
Foods cooked												
Meat	+	+	+	+		+	+					
Oil, fat	+	+	+	+		+						
Fish	+	+	+	+		+						
Method of use												
Hot stones only			+						+			
Over embers						+						
Beside flames							+	+				
Over flames							+					
Described as:												
"crumply"							+		+			
"crude"								+				
"heavy"							+					
"thick"										+	+	+
"easily broken"		+	+		+							
"water soluble"						+						
"spoils in wet weather"		+										
"poorly fired"			+									
"hardened by use"												+

Figure 10.1 Model showing the general relationship of performance and preservation properties of clay pots across low firing thresholds.

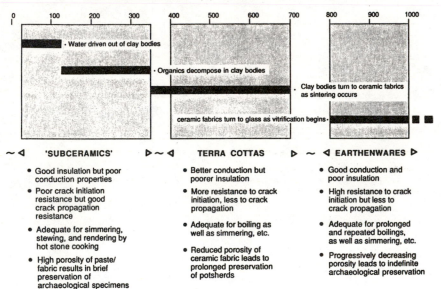

SOME THERMAL THRESHOLDS (C) IN HUNTER GATHERER POTTERY

· Water driven out of clay bodies

· Organics decompose in clay bodies

· Clay bodies turn to ceramic fabrics as sintering occurs

ceramic fabrics turn to glass as vitrification begins ·

~ ◁ 'SUBCERAMICS' ▷ ~ ◁ TERRA COTTAS ▷ ~ ◁ EARTHENWARES ▷

- Good insulation but poor conduction properties
- Poor crack initiation resistance but good crack propagation resistance
- Adequate for simmering, stewing, and rendering by hot stone cooking
- High porosity of paste/ fabric results in brief preservation of archaeological specimens

- Better conduction but poorer insulation
- More resistance to crack initiation, less to crack propagation
- Adequate for boiling as well as simmering, etc.
- Reduced porosity of ceramic fabric leads to prolonged preservation of potsherds

- Good conduction and poor insulation
- High resistance to crack initiation but less to crack propagation
- Adequate for prolonged and repeated boilings, as well as simmering, etc.
- Progressively decreasing porosity leads to indefinite archaeological preservation

PERFORMANCE AND PRESERVATION PROPERTIES OF CLAY COOKING POTS

PART FIVE

The Archaeologist and the Archaeometrician: Larger Questions

11

A Research Design for Ceramic Use-Wear Analysis at Grasshopper Pueblo

Michael B. Schiffer
Department of Anthropology, University of Arizona

Introduction

This paper outlines a program of use-wear analysis applicable to the rich ceramic assemblage from Grasshopper Ruin, a late Mogollon pueblo in east-central Arizona. The purpose of presenting this research design is to promote the development of general principles and techniques for ceramic use-wear analysis. This line of research is grounded in the emerging view that regards "pots as tools" (Braun 1983), that is, containers involved in the performance of concrete activities. By first understanding these activities, the archaeologist can improve the rigor of all inferences based on ceramic artifacts. The methods to be used in the proposed research draw inspiration from lithic studies, a field in which there has been much progress in inferring behavior from use-wear traces. The proposed use-wear analysis will specifically test the hypothesis—widely held by Southwestern archaeologists–that similar vessel forms of different wares and types had similar utilitarian functions (techno-functions).

In the past two decades, archaeologists have made remarkable strides in developing principles and procedures for drawing behavioral inferences from chipped stone and ceramic artifacts. Generally, these analytic studies fall into three broad (but not exhaustive) categories: (1) technology, (2) style, and (3) techno-function. In lithic studies, research in all three

Acknowledgments: I thank J. Jefferson Reid, Stephanie M. Whittlesey, and James M. Skibo for help in preparing this research design.

areas has moved ahead briskly. Even lithic "styles" have come under
intensive scrutiny in recent years, with intriguing results (for a limited
review, see Sackett 1982). In ceramic analyses, research on technology
continues to be productive, and many new avenues are being explored
(e.g., Olin and Franklin 1982; Rye 1981; Rice 1984). The traditional
mainstay of ceramic analysis—style—is experiencing a renaissance in
some areas; new techniques are vigorously attacking stylistic variability
in fruitful ways (for partial views, see Plog 1980, 1983). In comparison
to technology and style, investigations of ceramic techno-functions (i.e.,
use in activities) have lagged. Although ceramic specialists have called
for such studies for several decades (e.g., Matson 1965; Shepard 1965),
only a small number had been carried out until very recently (e.g., the
papers in Nelson 1984; Smith 1983; Braun 1983; Hally 1986; Steponaitis
1983; Bronitsky 1986; Henrickson and McDonald 1983).

Research on techno-functions will expand greatly in the next few
years as archaeologists strive to explore this major frontier of ceramic
analysis. In developing ceramic techno-functional—particularly use-wear—
analysis, archaeologists can and should draw general methodological
insights from analogous lithic studies, which are far advanced in this
area.

In addition to closing a logical set of research options, there are
important, long-standing reasons for archaeologists to develop rigorous
methods for studying ceramic techno-functions. First of all, inferences
on many topics, such as settlement systems, site functions, and activity
areas, require the use of techno-functional topologies for all recovered
artifacts. To date, very gross ceramic categories (i.e., bowls and jars or
decorated and undecorated) have been employed, especially in the
American Southwest (e.g., Plog 1980; Goodyear 1975; Doelle 1976). In
some cases, this low-level behavioral resolution is adequate; in other
cases, more precise specification of techno-functions is required. Thus,
improvements in techno-functional inference will lead to improvements
in higher-level behavioral and organizational inferences.

Second, some archaeologists have recently sought to investigate relationships between the attributes of pots and their mechanical performance characteristics (see Braun 1983 and Bronitsky 1986 and references
therein; Schiffer and Skibo 1987; Bronitsky and Hamer 1986; Steponaitis
1983). Clearly, the degree that one can rigorously evaluate the suitability
of various pottery types for carrying out specific tasks depends on how
well techno-function can be ascertained independently of performance
characteristics. For example, to avoid circularity in arguments, one must
know how a jar was used (e.g., for repeated heating of a liquid over
an open fire) before assessing how well its mechanical properties would
have permitted it to carry out that techno-function. As more is learned

about the relationships between techno-function and performance characteristics, it may become possible to infer the former from the latter.
Thus, advances in techno-functional inference will contribute to the
important and growing interest in understanding how and why pots
were produced with particular performance characteristics.

Third, better understanding of ceramic techno-functions will lead to
more sophisticated interpretations of stylistic variability. As Braun
(1983:113) has noted,

> the kinds of social information conveyable by an artifact, and hence the
> kinds of decoration they are likely to receive, vary with the artifact's size
> and its context in the social environment. . . . As a result, differential
> functional classes of vessel can receive different kinds of decoration (Plog
> 1980:17–19, 85–98). . . . In addition, even within a single functional class
> of vessels, vessels of different sizes may receive different decorative
> treatments according to their possibly different contexts of use.

In analyzing an assemblage of artifacts, such as lithics or ceramics, it
is generally believed that a techno-functional variability should first be
held constant to facilitate isolation of purely stylistic variability (cf.
Binford 1965; Jelinek 1976; Meltzer 1981). Indeed, some go so far as to
define style as the nonadaptive variability left behind when techno-
function is extracted (cf. Dunnell 1978). However, McGuire (1981) has
theoretically questioned this "residual" model of style, thereby implying
that stylistic analysis can proceed—at least in some cases—without a
thorough understanding of techno-functional variability. McGuire's arguments may be persuasive on a theoretical level, but cannot be op-
erationalized at present on ceramic and stone artifacts without recourse
to some version of the residual model. Indeed, by asserting that one is
dealing exclusively with stylistic variability, implicit claims are also being
made that (1) other variability is not stylistic and (2) other causes of
variability are not contributing to that portion of the variability labeled
as stylistic. As Sackett (1982:68) notes,

> function and style are most profitably viewed as full complementary aspects
> which, once the effects of post-depositional alteration have been accounted
> for, share equal responsibility for *all* formal variation observable in artifacts;
> also, the nature of these aspects is such that neither can be comprehended
> except in terms of the other.

Clearly, in the analytical process, the operations of isolating one type
of variability are done with respect to knowledge of the other. In view
of this relationship, one must conclude that a greater understanding of

ceramic techno-function can lead to improved analyses of stylistic variability.

For most analyses, archaeologists have been content to equate techno-function with gross morphological categories, such as bowl and jar. Although investigators may believe that techno-function is thereby held constant or taken into account, it is not. The following sections argue why this is so, and thus demonstrate an urgent need, especially in the American Southwest, for development of new methods for inferring ceramic techno-functions. Later sections will propose research to address this need.

Ceramic Variability in the American Southwest

Ceramic studies have long been the trademark of Southwestern archaeology. Beginning a century ago, scholars of every theoretical persuasion—e.g., Cushing (1886), Spier (1917), Kidder and Amsden (1931), Amsden (1936), Wheat et al. (1958), Breternitz (1966), Carlson (1970), Smith (1971), Longacre (1970), Hill (1970), Plog (1980), Washburn (1977), Graves (1982), Zaslow (1980)—have used "stylistic" variability to offer inferences on a bewildering array of subjects, from microtemporal change to marital residence pattern. In view of this intensive activity, it is surprising that the most fundamental question about ceramic variability remains unanswered: Why are there so many ceramic types in the Southwest? Indeed, the question is seldom asked.

Before addressing this question, one must rule out the possibility that the plethora of types results from the idiosyncracies of Southwestern archaeologists. Are the latter apt to be extreme splitters? Although Southwesternists have not been reluctant to proliferate types, a case can be made that most of the defined types do possess culture-historical validity and analytical utility; that is, the variability that they codify is related to time and/or space. For example, St. Johns Polychrome and Four Mile Polychrome were made, used, and deposited during different time periods over differing territories (Carlson 1970; Graves 1982). The occurrence of such ceramic types in undatable assemblages furnishes temporal information not otherwise obtainable. Thus, by the principal criterion of time/space distinctiveness, Southwestern types are not overdiscriminated.

Moreover, recent research suggests that a great deal of temporal variability remains within existing types. At present, however, the intellectual atmosphere in Southwestern archaeology discourages creation of new types. As a result, subdivision of existing types into varieties takes place under the more acceptable rubric of attribute seriation (cf. Plog 1980; LeBlanc 1975; Wallace 1986). For example, in the Hohokam area efforts are underway to distinguish finer divisions of the Red-on-buff series to facilitate more precise temporal control. Indeed, Haury and his students have recognized *de facto* types such as "Late Santa Cruz Red-on-buff" and "Early Sacaton Red-on-buff" for decades (E. W. Haury, personal communication, 1980). Presumably, attribute-based numerical methods will eventually succeed in providing an operational basis for distinguishing such varieties in the highly polythetic Hohokam buffware types. Similarly, recent work on early Anasazi black-on-white types furnishes grounds for defining additional varieties having temporal significance (e.g., Jernigan 1982). Symmetry analysis of pottery design (e.g., Zaslow 1980; Washburn 1977) may provide another basis for subdividing extant types.

Clearly, despite a half century of codifying Southwestern ceramic variability into types, that variability has by no means been exhausted—even within a culture-historical framework. The inescapable conclusion from all this research is that the prehistoric artisans of the Southwest generated a richly variegated ceramic tradition.

Rather than deal with this entire ceramic corpus, I have singled out for attention the ceramic variability (i.e., number of types) present at one point in time, in one community—Grasshopper (Reid 1974; Longacre et al. 1982). In many ways, this synchronic variability is the most surprising. It appears early in the Southwest, long before any traces of non-egalitarian societies are manifest. By the latest phases of prehistory, in the 13th–15th centuries, dozens of pottery-types—and several wares—were often present at one settlement, many of them demonstrably in use at the same time (as shown by associations in de facto refuse and burial assemblages). For example, at Grasshopper Pueblo, one finds four major wares and several dozen types, most of which were used contemporaneously. Similarly, during the Hohokam early Classic period, as illustrated by burial lots and de facto refuse at the Escalante Ruins, the types of Gila Red (Smudged and Unsmudged varieties), Gila Plain, Casa Grande Red-on-buff, and others, were in use at the same time (Doyel 1974).

Two generic hypotheses are invoked, implicitly, by Southwestern archaeologists to account for such variability. The first stresses that different types were used in different activities. In particular, decorated types were used differently than undecorated types. Thus, corrugated types were used for cooking and grain storage, and painted types were used for serving and water storage (cf. Plog 1980:83). These hypotheses are plausible, and receive some support from ethnographic data (Plog 1980; Smith 1983; Henrickson and McDonald 1983). Nevertheless, gross techno-functional hypotheses can only account—in very general terms—for *some* of the ceramic variability. Most of the really puzzling variability in types remains unexplained. For example, why were *decorated* bowls of Gila Polychrome, Grasshopper Polychrome, and Four Mile Polychrome of similar sizes in use at the same time? If one assumes that form and techno-function are highly correlated, an assumption that is the starting point for almost all ceramic analyses (e.g., Plog 1980:18), then it can only be concluded that bowls of identical shape and size—but of different types—had the same techno-functions. I submit that this is not necessarily the case.

The second type of hypothesis that purports to explain the remaining variability usually invokes various social processes, principally trade. However, a trade "explanation" is not an explanation for why *particular* types were traded. It is implicit in trade arguments that traded vessels carried out distinctive social functions in the recipient societies, but these functions are not specified. The following more specific hypotheses are among the possibilities: (1) different types were used by different social groups for the same activities, (2) different types were used by different social groups for different activities, and (3) different types were used by the same social group for different activities. Clearly, *differences in social functions may involve differences in activities* (techno-function). Thus, rigorous testing of socio-functional hypotheses requires a variety of contextual data (e.g., associations in de facto refuse and in burial lots) and, most importantly, information on techno-function derived from evidence in addition to shape and size (since the latter are often the same for different types.)

To deal realistically with synchronic variability in types, one must regard all vessels as facilities that could (and probably did) carry out both utilitarian and symbolic functions (*sensu* McGuire 1981; see also Rathje and Schiffer 1982; Sackett 1982). The most sacred bowl sometimes has contents and is moved about in ritual, while the most mundane cooking vessel can convey social information about its maker or user. Clearly, the first and most important step in understanding synchronic ceramic variability is to identify the utilitarian functions of all vessels, and to compare these functions among the different types. For example, were large bowls of Four Mile Polychrome, Grasshopper Polychrome, and Gila Polychrome used in the same way? Were they interchangeable stylistic variants in the same complex of activities or were they in fact used differently? These are the questions that need to be addressed if higher-level inferences and explanations about social relationships are to be made credible. Simply identifying a ceramic type as a "trade ware" does not explain why it was procured or how it functioned in the recipient society. We need to learn its mode of use in relation to other types.

Approaches to Inferring Ceramic Techno-function

As noted above, the most common way archaeologists infer ceramic techno-function is to assume that form and techno-function are intimately related. Indeed, our most basic formal terminology (e.g., bowl, jar) is infused with techno-functional inferences. Beginning with Linton (1944), investigators have increasingly refined these form-function relationships (correlates). Recent work (e.g., Smith 1983; Henrickson and McDonald 1983) has brought us to the verge of genuine theory regarding the mutual dependence of form and techno-function in ceramic artifacts. Other investigators have developed refined systems for describing ceramic forms (Ericson et al. 1972; Shepard 1965). We shall draw extensively upon the results of form-function studies, for form must be used as a basic famework for recording use-wear traces. However, for a number of reasons already noted, it is expected that potentially important variation in techno-function occurs *within* identical form classes.

In addition to the formal properties of vessel shape and size, analysis of residues—*on* and *in* sherds and vessels—can supply valuable information on pottery techno-function (e.g., Condamin et al. 1976; Duma 1972; Lucas 1962; Clancey 1961). Although residue analysis merits serious attention and continued refinement, it will not be a component of this research (with the exception of sooting).

Another approach that can answer questions about techno-function is ceramic use-wear analysis. It has the singular advantage of being applicable to all pots, washed or not, and is based on readily observed mechanical alterations. Regrettably, few detailed ceramic use-wear analyses have been published to date (e.g., Griffiths 1978; Hally 1983; Bray 1982); only one of these (Bray 1982) deals with Southwestern materials. Because ceramic use-wear research has not developed very far, I shall turn to lithic use-wear analysis for methodological inspiration.

Methodological Insights from Lithic Use-Wear Analysis

Two decades ago, the number of lithic use-wear analyses published in English-speaking countries could be counted on both hands. Several books on the topic have now appeared (Hayden 1979; Keeley 1980; Vaughan 1985), and major works are regularly published in journals and monographs. Progress in the experimental and technical realms of lithic use-wear analysis has been made at a rapid pace, leading sometimes to advances in our understanding of prehistory. A number of conclusions can be drawn from the recent spate of excellent work in lithic use-wear analysis that should be applicable to techno-functional analysis of other—especially ceramic—materials.

The first conclusion is that techno-functional analyses require the study of both artifact morphology (i.e., shape and size) and actual traces of wear. Obviously, artifacts can be manufactured for one activity but used in others. Moreover, form-function correlates often are weakly grounded and can incorrectly stereotype techno-function. For example, use-wear studies indicate that some Archaic and Paleoindian "projectile points" were sometimes used as bifacial knives (e.g., Ahler 1971). Here, form alone is an inadequate indicator of techno-function. In the study of ceramic functions, the establishment of generic form-function correlates is an important and timely line of research, but it furnishes—at best—only a convenient starting point for comprehensive techno-functional analyses. In ceramic studies, no less than in lithics, actual examination of use-wear traces is essential for inferring specific techno-functions.

A second important conclusion is that not all post-manufacture mechanical modifications on artifacts are traces of use (for summaries, see Keeley 1980; Odell 1982; Vaughan 1985). For example, lithic microflakes can result from a host of processes, ranging from trampling to museum curation practices. Similarly, ceramics—especially sherds—are altered by many processes, including reuse (e.g., Stanislawski 1969), burning, trampling, fluvial transport, and archaeological recovery and laboratory processes (cf. Schiffer 1983, 1987). Some of these processes may produce traces that mimic those modifications expected from actual use. Unfortunately, experimental study of these traces, which are mostly produced by formation processes, is only now beginning. I expect that these investigations will eventually disclose microscopic differences in seemingly identical traces. However, lack of sufficient research in this area places some constraints on what can be accomplished today in ceramic use-wear analysis. Clearly, assigning the damage on individual *sherds* to use or to particular formation processes is difficult. Accordingly, at present it is advisable to confine ceramic use-wear analyses to whole or restored vessels, where the placement of damage patterns over the vessel furnishes an additional line of evidence (Bray 1982; Hally 1983) for segregating traces of use from those of other processes. For example, the distribution of soot over a vessel's surface permits one to distinguish between use-wear and post-use burning. Fortunately, there are many whole vessel collections from important and well studied sites such as Grasshopper that are ideally suited to ceramic use-wear analysis. Thus, investigations into ceramic techno-function—those based on whole vessels—are not utterly dependent on breakthroughs in research on the traces of formation processes.

A third conclusion is that the use process itself must be conceived broadly to include the host of specific agencies and different settings that contribute directly and indirectly to the observed alteration patterns.

Let us deal with the simplest case: an artifact used for a single purpose. For example, a biface used as a butchering knife may acquire a polish in the haft area deriving from friction during use. On the blade of the same artifact, one also finds "meat polish" (*sensu* Keeley 1980), microflaking caused by occasional contact with bone, and striations left by abrasive particles from the working environment. Cleaning the knife after use, perhaps back at the base camp, and resharpening also contribute to the traces of "use."

Insights into the complexity of the use process gained from lithic studies are also applicable to ceramic artifacts. A cooking pot used over an open fire provides an example. The heating itself produces color changes and the deposition of soot and resins on the vessel's exterior (Hally 1983). Alternate heating and cooling may also contribute to thermal shock, which may be manifest in extreme cases by cracking or exfoliation of the vessel's surface (cf. Bronitsky and Hammer 1986). If the pot sits on stone "pot rests," then abrasions and nicks should be evidenced on the base and lower margin of the pot (Welch 1984). If ladles are used for serving, then the vessel's rim should be abraded and chipped from occasional, inadvertent contact. Similarly, the ladling should produce zones of abrasion and striations on the interior of the vessel. If the cooking pot is stored in the vicinity of the hearth when not in use, it will be subject to accidental contact and additional exterior damage. When the pot is cleaned, depending on the particular maintenance activities, additional traces will accumulate on the interior, and perhaps rim and exterior as well.

The many ways that traces may originate during use is not a liability in ceramic use-wear studies, but rather a decided asset. The richness of the traces and their sources produces characteristic patterns of wear that should distinguish—perhaps uniquely—particular uses within and between form/decoration classes.

In offering hypotheses to account for wear patterns, one must recall that sequential uses (e.g., secondary use), and multiple, alternating uses can also contribute to the overall patterns of observed wear (Schiffer 1979). Unlike chipped-stone artifacts, however, the traces of secondary use and multiple uses may not obscure earlier damage patterns. On pots that have not been recycled, traces of the earliest uses are often preserved. Each use contributes, cumulatively, to the observed use-wear pattern.

A final aspect of use that influences use wear is the total amount of activity in which the vessel participated (cf. Vaughan 1985). A new vessel, used little, should display only slight traces of wear, and these perhaps not at all distinctive. On the other hand, old, extensively used vessels should reveal a great deal of use wear (see Bray 1982). Comparison of early- and late-stage wear patterns within form/decoration classes should be instructive. For example, one might expect a series of vessels that were used in the same tasks to exhibit gradual, sequential development of damage patterns; if this expectation is not met, then multiple or sequential development of damage patterns; if this expectation is not met, then multiple or sequential uses might be responsible. Multiple uses, for example, should lead to extreme variability in early-stage wear patterns. Sequential uses should result in divergent trajectories, with later-stage vessels exhibiting excessive variability. In any event, "total amount of use" is an important variable that affects use-wear patterns. Together with wear patterns themselves, the amount of wear furnishes evidence on mode of use.

The fourth conclusion from lithic use-wear analysis is that a precise language for describing damage must be developed as soon as practicable. Lithic use-wear research has now progressed to the point where agreement has been reached on terminology in some areas (e.g., kinds of polish—Vaughan 1985); in other areas, such as the most economical way to describe the locations of wear, much remains to be done. So little work has been accomplished to date in ceramic use-wear analysis that opportunities for terminological confusion have not yet arisen. In order to minimize the effort that will be necessarily devoted at some later date to standardizing terminology, all investigators should strive to be as explicit as possible about terms and definitions, seeking when possible descriptions that have universal applicability. In addition, types of wear and wear patterns should be extensively documented photographically—at both microscopic and macroscopic scales.

The fifth and final conclusion that can be transferred from lithic to ceramic use-wear analysis concerns the role of the mechanical properties of the material in the production of wear. For example, it is generally known that obsidian, chert, quartzite, and basalt wear differently. Investigators are now beginning to apply standardized tests to quantify these different properties (e.g., Greiser and Sheets 1979). There is every reason to believe that differences in paste, temper, surface treatment, and firing temperature of ceramics will give rise to similar variability in performance characteristics relating to use, such as resistance to chipping and resistance to abrasion. For example, Vaz Pinto et al. (1987) have shown that temper type and quantity influence abrasion resistance (see also Skibo and Schiffer 1987). We would expect pots differing in performance characteristics to display differences in use wear, even if they were subjected to identical uses. Techno-functional studies of ceramics are already beginning to investigate how, for example, potters manipulate temper and surface treatment to alter performance characteristics. It remains to extend this emphasis to ceramic use-wear analysis so that one can demonstrate that differences in wear patterns result from different uses, not different performance characteristics of the vessels.

In developing standardized tests for Grasshopper ceramics, we shall draw upon the extensive literature in materials science on modern ceramics (for an introduction, see Bronitsky 1986). There is an ongoing concern in this field with the effects of manufacturing processes on product function, reliability, and durability. However, it will be necessary to develop new tests, appropriate for archaeological ceramics, that are behaviorally relevant (Schiffer and Skibo 1987).

Proposed Research

The Grasshopper Test Case

The development of general principles and techniques for ceramic use-wear analysis will be carried out on the pottery assemblage from Grasshopper Pueblo. Grasshopper is a 500-room masonry pueblo in east-central Arizona. Extensive excavations carried out at this site during the past two decades have produced an assemblage that may be unique in terms of the number of whole vessels recovered with thoroughly documented provenience. The assemblage includes 889 mortuary pots and approximately 800 room-floor vessels (J.J. Reid, personal communication, 1984); many of the latter remain to be reconstructed.

The Grasshopper ceramic assemblage is ideal for the purposes of this study for several reasons: (1) the large number of whole and restorable vessels, which thoroughly sample the range of ceramic variation, (2) the considerable number of different wares and types that comprise the assemblage and that were used contemporaneously, (3) the likely existence of use-wear traces on the majority of vessels, (4) the extensive number of problem-oriented studies already carried out on Grasshopper materials, which furnish a solid foundation for the use-wear analysis, and (5) previous studies of Grasshopper ceramics have given rise to a number of intriguing hypotheses that can be tested by use-wear analysis.

This last point should be amplified to underscore the importance of carrying out this exploratory use-wear analysis on a well studied assemblage. Researchers have been investigating whole-vessel distributions in burials and have begun examining floor assemblages (de facto refuse), with important results. In an early analysis, Mauer (1970) discovered that Cibecue Polychrome vessels occurred almost exclusively in grave lots. This pattern has been confirmed recently on a larger sample of whole vessels (Reid 1984), warranting the hypothesis that Cibecue Polychrome may have been manufactured for use in mortuary rituals. Whittlesey (n.d.) discovered in a preliminary inspection that child burials accompanied by one decorated pottery type tend to have different wares present (i.e., White Mountain, Grasshopper, or Salado) in different parts of the pueblo. These spatial patterns may signal the existence of residence groups or some other major social division in the community. Curiously, white wares do not exhibit any simple spatial patterns but do appear to have gender relationships. The richest burial recovered to date, a man inferred to have held leadership positions in at least two ceremonial associations, was buried with all the major decorated types as well as Cibecue Polychrome, Salado Red, and Corrugated types. Distribution patterns of wares in house floor assemblages are still being investigated, but do not appear to display such definite associational or spatial patterning (S. Whittlesey, personal communication, 1984).

The social differences in ceramics hinted at by these archaeological patterns furnish a number of hypotheses that can be examined by use-wear analysis. For example, if Cibecue Polychrome had been used primarily in mortuary ritual, then most vessels should exhibit little wear. Mauer (1970), in an early study using a small sample of vessels, found this to be the case. If the major wares were indeed associated symbolically with different social groups, carrying out basically the same activities, then equivalent form classes should display similar wear patterns.

Methods

In the course of evaluating the above hypotheses, the proposed research will develop and test a rigorous and replicable approach for the analysis of ceramic use-wear using the Grasshopper collection. The study will consist of the following, largely sequential components.

1. A sample (several hundred) of Grasshopper whole vessels will be examined in order to develop a descriptive system for recurrent types of wear. Experiments on sherds and on modern pots will augment those observations.

Previous inspections of whole vessels for traces of mechanical wear by the author indicate that a considerable degree of complexity is present in specific use-wear traces and in their patterns of occurrence on vessels. Thus, several levels of observation are required for recording use wear. The most basic level consists of the smallest identifiable traces, or *marks*— a single scratch, nick, or chip—that seem to be the product of one event. Marks occur in more-or-less distinct varieties, depending on both the nature of the contact (e.g., static or dynamic loading, oblique or normal angle of incidence) and its placement on the vessel. It should be noted that not all marks appear to be caused by mechanical contact. For example, some marks—best described as "pits"—are occasionally found over the entire surface of a painted vessel. Close inspection reveals that these pits, which resemble pot lids on burned stone, were created by spalling from the interior not contact. One possibility is that a temper particle expanded, pushing out a hertzian cone; bits produced in this manner are also common in historic and recent Acoma pottery. It is important that such pits not be confused with marks produced by use wear.

Kinematic principles (relating to motions of use) developed in lithic use-wear analysis (e.g., Semenov 1964) can aid in the designation of specific types of behaviorally significant marks. For example, marks such as scratches and sometimes nicks have orientations that indicate the direction from which contact originated. Thus, differences in angle of contact and direction of motion produce differences in the size or orientation of marks that may be consequential for behavioral inference. Using established principles, and supplementing these where necessary with our experiments, we shall strive to identify the types of marks most useful for behavioral inference. Provisional classifications of marks will be refined and tested against the corpus of whole vessels.

The second level of observation is groups of marks or *patches*. A patch is the result of repeated contact of a similar nature in the same general area. However, patches may contain more than one type of mark. For example, jar rims often display patches containing scratches and chips.

Patches also vary in size and morphology, and these characteristics should furnish an excellent index to the overall amount of use experienced by a vessel. The following scenario provides a general model for the development of some types of patch. A portion of a vessel subjected to repeated contact in the same manner will at first exhibit a number of marks. At this stage, the formation of a definite patch may not be evident, especially if the marks apparently occur at random over the vessel. However, continued use will lead to the accumulation of additional marks to the extent that their clustering finally becomes obvious. At this stage, each mark is still distinct, and its size and orientation can be observed. Further use results in extensive overlaying of marks, causing the patch to become differentiated into a *center* and *periphery*. The center displays extensive removal of the vessel's surface, extending below the slip or surface treatment, and exposing paste and temper to further damage. Most marks in the center are not longer distinctive. In some cases, patches have multiple centers. The periphery of a patch retains distinctive marks.

As wear continues, the center of the patch grows, usually at the expense of the periphery. Clearly, a simple index to the gross amount of wear (and possibly the gross amount of use in a particular task) is the area covered by the patch's center. Because of differences in contact processes, not all patches conform to the above scenario. For example, on some small "flower pot" bowls of the Grasshopper, the base exhibits a large patch of reduced surface reflectance ("dulling"); neither a periphery nor distinct marks are visible to the naked eye. This type of patch probably results from extended contact with soft materials or unconsolidated sand. Clearly, experiments and microscopic examination will be necessary to clarify the nature and origin of such patches. Other patches have multiple or discontinuous areas of wear. In some vessels, an undulating surface is responsible for the pattern; other cases are more problematic.

Description of a patch involves specification of overall size, size of the center(s), kinds of marks in the periphery (if any), and location on the vessel. Although we do not plan to ignore isolated marks, the characteristics of patches will probably furnish the most consistently interpretable evidence on techno-function.

Both marks and patches occur in spatial patterns on vessels. For example, my preliminary inspection of the Grasshopper collections revealed that some narrow-mouth jars exhibit a patch of chips on the exterior of the rim. Many "ollas" display patches consisting of nicks and scratches on the widest part of the exterior. These spatial patterns provide essential information about techno-function. For example, if patches are highly localized on one side of a vessel, the vessel may have been stationary, since one would not expect a radially symmetrical vessel to have a preferred orientation during use. In recording both marks and patches, this all-important spatial patterning will be preserved.

In recording and studying marks and patches care will be taken to distinguish use-wear from traces of post-use processes insofar as possible. Because most Grasshopper whole vessels were reassembled from sherds, one has a ready-made test for pre- versus post-breakage damage. Marks and patches that abruptly halt on the margin of a sherd and do not continue to the adjacent sherd were probably produced by post-breakage processes. In particular, some nicks seem to be confined to the edge of sherds, suggesting, perhaps, damage during recovery. Similarly, on the smudged interior of one bowl, striations on adjacent sherds were oriented in different directions, clearly implicating abrasive processes during cleaning. Using sherds and pots fabricated in our laboratory, we will carry out the experiments needed to investigate the origin of specific damage patterns.

In addition to marks and patches are alterations known as sooting. A deposit of a dark, carbon-rich organic residue on the surface of a vessel (see Hally 1983), sooting is present on many vessels in the Grasshopper collection. As Hally (1983) notes, the distribution of sooting on a vessel is usually highly patterned and often points directly to the nature of a vessel's use. For example, Kobayashi (1984) studied sooting patterns on the Mogollon vessels known as "plates." On many examples of this vessel, he found a distinctive ring of sooting just inside the rim of the upper, incurved surface. On the basis of this recurrent pattern of sooting, Kobayashi suggests that these "plates" were in fact lids for cooking pots. No other use would appear to account as economically for the distinctive sooting pattern. In view of this significant information potential, sooting patterns on the Grasshopper vessels will be sought and recorded meticulously.

The sample of whole vessels to be studied will be selected using stratified design so as to include examples from all parts of the pueblo. In that way, hypotheses about the social correlates of vessel usage patterns can be evaluated with an independent (spatial) line of evidence.

At the close of Component 1 we will have produced a photographically documented typology of behaviorally significant use-wear traces.

2. *Development of appropriate formal typology for Grasshopper whole vessels.*

This component will establish the framework of formal variation in terms of which use wear will be recorded. By formal variation is meant attributes of decoration, shape, and size. In comparing use-wear patterns among decorative types (e.g., Four Mile Polychrome vs. Grasshopper Polychrome), it will be necessary to hold constant those attributes— principally vessel shape and size—that are clearly related to techno-function. For example, we would expect the largest Four Mile Polychrome bowls to differ in use—and therefore in use wear—from the smallest. We will be able to employ established Southwestern wares and types as well as shape classes. Behaviorally significant variation in vessel size must still be examined. Frequency distributions of size for each shape class (within decorative types) will be examined to facilitate the derivation of appropriate size classes. Formal attributes of size to be recorded include weight, volume, height, maximum width, and interior orifice diameter.

3. *Quantitative assessment of performance characteristics of Grasshopper ceramics using a sample of sherds.*

All types of ceramics, even modern porcelain and stoneware, accumulate use-wear traces, but the low-fired products of traditional potters in the Southwest are especially vulnerable to damage during use. However, not all ceramic types were equally susceptible to wear. Thus, holding constant size and shape, vessels will exhibit differences in use-wear patterns depending on their performance characteristics, such as resistance to abrasion and resistance to chipping. Moreover, there is no reason to believe *a priori* that a ceramic type resistant to one type of wear will also exhibit high resistance to another type. In addition to establishing

comparability between ceramic types, testing of performance characteristics will furnish evidence for evaluating the suitability of particular
types for carrying out specific techno-functions. For this reason, tests
on porosity and permeability, which are not directly related to the
production of use-wear traces, will also be carried out.

The most efficient way to document variability in performance characteristics is to subject sherd samples to standardized testing procedures.
Recently, a number of testing procedures have been applied to prehistoric
ceramics in various techno-functional studies (e.g., Bronitsky 1986). At
the present time, however, standardized tests for wear-related performance
characteristics have not been applied to archaeological ceramics.

Final selection of properties to be measured and machines to be
fabricated or purchased will be made after the completion of Component
1. At the present time, however, the following tentative choices can be
outlined.

A. A sizable number of use-wear marks are produced by abrasive
processes that leave scratches. Although many commercial testers have
been developed for quantifying abrasion resistance, few are well suited
for archaeological ceramics. The problems have become obvious as a
result of experiments carried out so far in our laboratory.

Primitive ceramics, with their vast amounts of heterogeneous, non-
plastic additive (temper), do not shear abrasively like homogeneous,
fine-paste ceramics. Thus, commercial testers applicable to the latter may
not adequately simulate wear processes of primitive ceramics. For example,
I once believed that the Dietert-Fargo Abrasion Tester would be suitable.
This device consists of a rubber wheel that spins in a slurry of sand.
A specimen is held at a constant force against the rotating wheel and
is abraded by sand particles adhering to the wheel. After a specified
number of rotations, the specimen is dried and the weight loss ascertained.
Like all grinding processes, the rate of material loss is conditioned by
the quantity and hardness of the most resistant constituents Thus, a
sherd with much quartz temper might fare well in this test, yet wear
poorly in use. Under conditions of actual use, the rate of abrasive wear
is also a function of the weakest constituent of the ceramic as well as
the strength of the bonds between constituents. Moreover, in low-fire
ceramics, many of the more resistant particles abrade little themselves,
but are eventually dislodged as the water surrounding matrix gives way.
This is readily observed on well developed patches formed by abrasive
processes; many of the harder temper particles, almost pedestalled,
adhere only tenuously to the vessel's surface.

We have been developing a family of tests that are more responsive
to the actual wear processes of the low-fired heterogeneous ceramics so
often found by archaeologists (Skibo 1987; Vaz Pinto et al. 1987; Skibo

and Schiffer 1987). These tests subject sherds to repeated contact with abrasive particles in a lapidary tumbler. Sherds to be tested are cut on a diamond saw to a standard size and the edges are ground flat and smooth. Before tumbling, the sherd is weighed to the nearest .001g. Test sherds can be tumbled wet or dry with a variety of abrasive particles ranging in size from fine sand to cobbles. After tumbling for a specified time period and drying, the sherd is reweighed and the percentage weight loss determined. Sherds with greater weight loss have less abrasion resistance (holding constant sherd thickness). By varying the abrasive material, it is possible to simulate a variety of use conditions. Indeed, the resemblance of the surface of test specimens to use-wear traces on actual archaeological sherds is uncanny.

B. A second major type of wear on ceramics is chipping on the rim and in other vulnerable areas (e.g., handles). Testing of chipping resistance will be carried out with a falling weight impact tester (Mabry et al. n.d.). This device permits steel ball bearings of different size to be dropped on specimens from varying heights. The falling distance needed to consistently produce chips on a 90 degree cut platform on test sherds will indicate chipping resistance.

C. Although most damage seems to be effected by abrasive and chipping processes, a number of marks are the result of unspecified processes that "nick" or indent the vessel, usually at non-normal angles to the surface. It appears that these marks are the result of impacts that fell short of the force needed to completely fracture the vessel. Our falling weight impact tester can be adapted to testing the performance characteristics of nick resistance. Small ball bearings will be dropped repeatedly on specimens from a great height, and the resultant damage assessed. Fewer and shallower nicks will indicate greater nick resistance.

D. Porosity and permeability will also be tested. Apparent porosity (cf. Bronitsky 1986) will be directly ascertained by measuring water uptake, under standardized conditions, per unit volume of test sherd. Permeability will be measured with a new device now under development in our laboratory. It will measure the rate at which water flows through a saturated sherd. (The simple water-drop test actually measures *absorption rate*, not permeability.)

Several general considerations will guide out development and application of testing procedures. First of all, sherd specimens will be cut and ground to standardized shapes and sizes, as appropriate for each test. Second, materials testing always produces a large spread of values (for some ceramic examples, see Shepard 1965), even with homogeneous materials. Thus, large sherd samples are sometimes needed to characterize the performance characteristics—expressed as a mean and standard deviation—of any ceramic type.

Another family of factors that influences the distribution of test values is post-breakage, noncultural formation processes (cf. Schiffer 1987). A variety of chemical and physical agents can be expected to degrade various performance characteristics of archaeological sherds. Among these are: (1) exposure to moisture and wet-dry cycles, (2) thermal cycling, (3) freeze-thaw cycling, and (4) salt erosion. In order to control for the effects of these processes, it will be necessary to obtain sherd samples from comparable depositional environments at Grasshopper such as the floors of late-abandoned rooms. Although this will insure that all sherds have been subjected to the *same* environmental processes, it cannot compensate for any differences in the inherent susceptibility of particular ceramic types to articular formation processes. We are optimistic—but by no means confident—that ceramics generally more durable in use will also be more durable in the depositional environment. Thus, we would not expect environmental processes ordinarily to alter the *relative* strengths of various ceramic types. Obviously, this is a questionable assumption, one that we will strive to test at every opportunity. In any event, the influence of environmental processes on test values also favors the use of large same sizes.

4. *Recording of use-wear traces on a stratified sample of Grasshopper whole vessels.*

The detailed non-destructive recording procedures, refined in Component 1, will be applied to a large sample of Grasshopper whole vessels using strata based on the formal types defined in Component 3. It is expected that some form classes will have few examples, whereas others will have many. To ensure adequate representation, sample sizes will be increased for low-frequency classes. In addition, sample sizes of abundant classes will be adjusted upward or downward—depending on the homogeneity in use-wear traces observed as the recording proceeds. For example, if a great deal of variability is found, sample size will be increased.

5. *Analysis of use-wear traces on Grasshopper whole vessels.*

The purpose of this analysis is to identify the basic structure of use wear in the Grasshopper assemblage. The first step will be to use various indices of overall wear, such as total area of patches, to rank the vessels within each form class. Second, information from the testing of performance characteristics will be used to assess the likelihood that the observed patterns—within and between form classes—are a product of differences in the wear resistance of the pottery. Third, evidence will be sought, in accord with previous hypotheses, for sequential and multiple uses. Fourth, behavioral hypotheses—i.e., specific techno-functions—will be advanced to account for the observed wear patterns within each form class. And, fifth, additional lines of evidence, including other traces of use and specific attributes of form, will be examined in order to evaluate the behavioral hypotheses.

6. *Function analysis of Grasshopper vessels.*

This effort will be directed toward the testing of higher-level behavioral hypotheses that specify functional differences between the form types. Of particular interest will be comparisons between analogous shapes (e.g., large bowls) in different style categories (e.g., Four Mile Polychrome vs. Gila Polychrome). On the basis of these comparisons, we shall attempt to present an empirical basis for characterizing ceramic function, including social functions. At the conclusion of this component, evidence should permit rigorous testing of the principal hypothesis, that similar vessel forms (of different types and wares) had similar techno-functions. We shall also incorporate spatial evidence in the testing of these hypotheses.

Conclusion

Understanding why Southwestern ceramics are so varied will take a concerted effort of many years. One way to contribute to that goal is by carrying out a thorough use-wear analysis of the important ceramic collection from Grasshopper Pueblo. With its many well documented whole and restored vessels and ancillary analyses that have already been conducted, Grasshopper furnishes an ideal starting point for the development of ceramic use-wear principles and techniques.

References Cited

Ahler, S.A. "Projectile Point Form and Function at Rodgers Shelter, Missouri." *Missouri Archaeological Society, Research Series 8.* 1971.

Amsden, C.A. "An Analysis of Hohokam Pottery Design." *Gila Pueblo, Medallion Paper 23.* 1936.

Binford, L.R. "Archaeological Systematics and the Study of Culture Process." *American Antiquity.* 32:203–210, 1965.

Braun, D.P. "Pots as Tools." in *Archaeological Hammers and Theories,* edited by J.A. Moore and A.S. Keene, pp. 107–134. Academic Press, New York, 1983.

Bray, A. "Mimbres Black-on-white, Melamine or Wedgewood? A Ceramic Use-wear Analysis." *The Kiva.* 47:133–149, 1982.

Breternitz, D.A. "An Appraisal of Tree-ring Dated Pottery Types in the Southwest." *University of Arizona, Anthropological Papers 10.* 1966.

Bronitsky, Gordon. "The Use of Materials Science Techniques in the Study of Pottery Construction and Use." in *Advances in Archaeological Method and Theory,* Vol. 9, edited by M.B. Schiffer, pp. 209–276. Academic Press, Orlando, 1986.

Bronitsky, Gordon, and Hamer, Robert. "Experiments in Ceramic Technology: The Effects of Various Tempering Materials on Impact and Thermal Shock Resistance." *American Antiquity.* 51:89–101, 1986.

Carlson, R.L. "White Mountain Redwares." *University of Arizona, Anthropological Papers 19.* 1970.

Clancey, J.J. "Chemical Analysis of Residue from an Indian Hill Ceramic Pot." *Massachusetts Archaeological Society, Bulletin.* 22:44–46, 1961.

Condamin, J., Formenti, F., Metais, M.O., Michel, M., and Blond, P. "The Application of Gas Chromatography to the Tracing of Oil in Ancient Amphorae." *Archaeometry.* 18:195–202, 1976.

Cushing, F.H. "A Study of Pueblo Pottery as Illustrative of Zuni Culture Growth." *Fourth Report of the Bureau of Ethnology.* pp. 467–521. Washington, D.C., 1886.

Doelle, W.H. "Desert Resources and Hohokam Subsistence: The Conoco Florence Project." *Arizona State Museum, Archaeological Series 103.* 1976.

Doyle, D. "Excavations in the Escalante Ruin Group, Southern Arizona." *Arizona State Museum, Archaeological Series 37.* 1974.

Duma, G. "Phosphate Content of Ancient Pots as Indication of Use." *Current Anthropology.* 13:127–129, 1972.

Dunnell, R.C. "Style and Function: A Fundamental Dichotomy." *American Antiquity.* 43:192–202, 1978.

Ericson, J.E., Read, D., and Burke, C. "Research Design: the Relationship between the Primary Functions and the Physical Properties of Ceramic Vessels and their Implications for Distributions on an Archaeological Site." *Anthropology UCLA.* 3:84–95, 1972.

Goodyear, A.C. "Hecla II and III: an Interpretive Study of Archaeological Remains from the Lakeshore Project, Papago Reservation, South-central Arizona." *Arizona State University, Anthropological Research Papers 9.* 1975.

Graves, M.W. "Breaking Down Ceramic Variation: Testing Models of White Mountain Redware Design Style Development." *Journal of Anthropological Archaeology.* 1:305–354, 1982.

Greiser, S.T. and Sheets, P.D. "Raw Materials as a Functional Variable in Use-wear Studies." in *Lithic Use-wear Analysis,* edited by B. Hayden, pp. 289–296. Academic Press, New York, 1979.

Griffiths, D.M. "Use-marks on Historic Ceramics: a Preliminary Study." *Historical Archaeology.* 12:68–81, 1978.

Hally, D.J. "Use Alteration of Pottery Vessel Surfaces: an Important Source of Evidence for the Identification of Vessel Function." *North American Archaeologist.* 4:3–26, 1983.

———. "The Identification of Vessel Function: a Case Study from Northwest Georgia." *American Antiquity.* 51:267–295, 1986.

Hayden, B. (editor) *Lithic Use-Wear Analysis.* Academic Press, New York, 1979.

Henrickson, R.F. and McDonald, M.M.A. "Ceramic Form and Function: an Ethnographic Search and an Archaeological Application." *American Anthropologist.* 85:630–643, 1983.

Hill, J.N. "Broken K Pueblo: Prehistoric Social Organization in the American Southwest." *University of Arizona, Anthropological Papers 18.* 1970.

Jelinek, A.J. "Form, Function, and Style in Lithic Analysis." in *Cultural Change and Continuity: Essays in Honor of James Bennett Griffin*, edited by C.E. Cleland, pp. 19–33. Academic Press, New York, 1976.

Jernigan, E.W. "The White Mount-Kiatuthlanna-Red Mesa Stylistic Tradition." in Cholla Project archaeology, Volume 5, Ceramic Studies, edited by J.J. Reid, pp. 39–427. *Arizona State Museum Archaeological Series 161.*, 1982.

Keeley, L.H. *Experimental Determination of Stone Tool Uses: a Microwear Analysis.* University of Chicago Press, Chicago, 1980

Kidder, A.V. and Amsden, C.A. *The Pottery of Pecos, Volume 1.* Phillips Academy, Andover, Massachusetts, 1931.

Kobayashi, Masashi. "Identification of Vessel Function: a Ceramic Use-wear Perspective." Ms. on file, Laboratory of Traditional Technology, Department of Anthropology, University of Arizona, 1984.

LeBlanc, S.A. "Micro-seriation: a Method for Fine Chronological Differentiation." *American Antiquity.* 40:22–38, 1975.

Linton, R. "North American Cooking Pots." *American Antiquity.* 9:369–380, 1944.

Longacre, W.A. "Archaeology as Anthropology: a Case Study." *University of Arizona, Anthropology Papers 17.* 1970.

Longacre, William A., Holbrook, Sally J., and Graves, Michael W. (editors) "Multidisciplinary Research at Grasshopper Pueblo, Arizona." *University of Arizona, Anthropological Papers 40.* 1982.

Lucas, A. *Ancient Egyptian Materials and Industries.* E. Arnold, London, 1962.

Mabry, Jonathan, Skibo, James M., Schiffer, Michael B., and Kvamme, Kenneth. "Use of a Falling Weight Impact Tester for Assessing Ceramic Impact Strength." *American Antiquity.* (in press, ms. 1987).

Matson, F.R. (editor) *Ceramics and Man.* Aldine, Chicago, 1965.

Mauer, M.D. "Cibecue Polychrome: a Fourteenth Century Ceramic Type from East-central Arizona." Unpublished M.A. Thesis, Department of Anthropology, University of Arizona, 1970.

McGuire, R.H. "A Consideration of Style in Archaeology." *University of Arizona Anthropology Club, Atlatl, Occasional Papers.* 2:13–29, 1981.

Meltzer, D.J. "A Study of Style and Function in a Class of Tools." *Journal of Field Archaeology.* 8:303–326, 1981.

Nelson, B.A. (editor) *Measurement and Explanation of Ceramic Variation: Some Current Examples.* Southern Illinois University Press, Carbondale, 1984.

Odell, G.L. "Emerging Directions in the Analysis of Prehistoric Tool Use." *Reviews in Anthropology.* 9:17–33, 1982.

Olin, J.S. and Franklin, A.D. (editors) *Archaeological Ceramics.* Smithsonian Institution Press, Washington, D.C., 1982.

Plog, Stephen. *Stylistic Variation in Prehistoric Ceramics.* Cambridge University Press, London, 1980.

———. "Analysis of Style in Artifacts." *Annual Review of Anthropology.* 12:125–142, 1983.

Rathje, W.L. and Schiffer, M.B. *Archaeology.* Harcourt Brace Jovanovich, New York, 1982.

Reid, J. Jefferson (editor) "Behavioral Archaeology at the Grasshopper Ruin." *The Kiva.* 40:1–112, 1974.

_____ . "What is Black-on-white and Vague All Over." in Regional analysis of prehistoric ceramic variation: contemporary studies of the Cibola Whitewares, edited by A.P. Sullivan and J.L. Hantman, pp. 135–152. *Arizona State University, Anthropological Research Papers 31.* 1984.

Rice, Prudence M. (editor) "Pots and Potters: Current Approaches in Ceramic Archaeology." *UCLA Institute of Archaeology, Monograph XXIV.* 1984.

Rye, O.S. *Pottery Technology.* Taraxacum, Washington, D.C., 1981.

Sackett, J.R. "Approaches to Style in Lithic Archaeology." *Journal of Anthropological Archaeology.* 1:59–112, 1982.

Schiffer, M.B. "The Place of Lithic Use-wear Studies in Behavioral Archaeology." in *Lithic Use-wear Analysis*, edited by Brian Hayden, pp. 15–25. Academic Press, New York, 1979.

_____ . "Toward the Identification of Formation Processes." *American Antiquity.* 48:675–706, 1983.

_____ . *Formation Processes of the Archaeological Record.* University of New Mexico Press, Albuquerque, 1987.

Schiffer, Michael B. and Skibo, James M. "Theory and Experiment in the Study of Technological Change." *Current Anthropology 28.* 1987.

Semenov, S.A. *Prehistoric Technology.* (Translated by M.W. Thompson). Cory, Adams, and Mackay, London, 1964.

Shepard, A.O. "Ceramics for the Archaeologist." *Carnegie Institution of Washington, Publication 609.* 1965.

Skibo, James M. "Fluvial Sherd Abrasion and the Interpretation of Surface Remains on Southwestern Bajadas." *North American Archaeologist.* 8:125–141, 1987.

Skibo, James M. and Schiffer, Michael B. "The Effects of Water on Processes of Ceramic Abrasion." *Journal of Archaeological Science.* 14:83–96, 1987.

Smith, M.F., Jr. "The Study of Ceramic Function from Artifact Size and Shape." Doctoral Dissertation, University of Oregon, University Microfilms, Ann Arbor, 1983.

Smith W. "Painted Ceramics of the Western Mound at Awatovi." *Peabody Museum of Archaeology and Ethnology, Papers 38.* 1971.

Spier, L. "An Outline for a Chronology of Zuni Ruins." *American Museum of Natural History, Anthropological Papers 18(4).* 1917.

Stanislawski, M.B. "What Good is a Broken Pot? An Experiment in Hopi-Tewa Ethno-archaeology." *Southwestern Lore.* 35:11–18, 1969.

Steponaitis, V. *Ceramics, Chronology, and Community Patterns: an Archaeological Study at Moundville.* Academic Press, New York, 1983.

Vaughan, Patrick C. *Use-wear Analysis of Flaked Stone Tools.* University of Arizona Press, Tucson, 1985.

Vaz Pinto, Ines, Schiffer, Michael B., Smith, Susan, and Skibo, James M. "Effects of Temper on Ceramic Abrasion Resistance: a Preliminary Investigation." *Archeomaterials.* 1:119–134, 1987.

Wallace, Henry D. "Decorated Ceramics." in Archaeological investigations at the Tanque Verde Wash site: a Middle Rincon settlement in the eastern Tucson basin, by Mark D. Elson, pp. 125– 180. *Institute for American Research, Anthropological Papers 7.* 1986.

Washburn, D.K. "A Symmetry Analysis of Upper Gila Area Ceramic Design." *Peabody Museum of Archaeology and Ethnology, Papers 68.*

Welch, John. "A Preliminary Study of the Life History Traces of Kalinga Ceramics." Ms. on file, Laboratory of Traditional Technology, Department of Anthropology, University of Arizona, 1984.

Wheat, J.B., Gifford, J.C., and Wasley, W.W. "Ceramic Variety, Type Cluster, and Ceramic System in Southwestern Pottery Analysis." *American Antiquity.* 24:34–47, 1958.

Whittlesey, Stephanie M. In preparation.

Zaslow, B. "Mirror Orientation in Hohokam Designs and the Chronology of Early Hohokam Phases." *The Kiva* 45:211–225, 1980.

12

Productive Specialization, Archaeometry, and Interpretation

Fred Plog and Steadman Upham

Department of Sociology and Anthropology,
New Mexico State University

Many archaeologists seem to believe that there are a battery of methods and techniques available for resolving nearly any pertinent archaeological problem. These are the chemical, biological, radiometric and physical techniques that are routinely used in the course of scientific research, both in archaeology and in other disciplines. There is, however, a growing recognition that these "archaeometries" do not always provide the required degree of precision to answer questions about the past nor do they, in some cases, even provide appropriate analytical frameworks. In this paper, we examine the role of archaeometric techniques in archaeological research and discuss the results of analyses we have undertaken over the past several years. While we are still favorably inclined toward the use of archaeometric analyses, we emphasize caution in the wholesale application of such techniques to the study of the past.

Archaeometry and Archaeological Research

During the past several years, we have had the opportunity to use a variety of archaeometric techniques in attempting to answer questions about specialized ceramic production and long distance exchange in the American Southwest. We believe that our use of these techniques has been productive and in this sense, the present paper in not a condemnation of their utility. We have, however, learned a variety of lessons from which we feel others might benefit. In one respect, the disappointment we presently feel is a direct result of our own naivete regarding the use of specific analytical technique and our failure to ask the appropriate questions of archaeometricians. In another potentially more important aspect, the disillusionment stems directly from archaeometricians over-estimating the power of particular techniques to resolve archaeological problems.

It is this latter issue that has prompted us to offer a definition of archaeometry. We feel that archaeometry refers not to a topic, to a body of specialized information, nor to a set of high-powered analytical techniques, but to both a structure and to roles. Coming from a discipline in which precise quantified procedures play only a limited part, all of those things that are said to be archaeometric involve attempts to describe more precisely and accurately attributes which archaeologists regard as essential to the resolution of some problem. In one sense, we can identify efforts such as these as attempts to go beyond "the eyeball." At the same time, what is familiar is not archaeometric. Whatever one's archaeological specialty, the archaeometry and the ensuing application of archaeometric techniques to archaeological problems that may ultimately contribute to a situation in which the non-archaeologist archaeometrician leads the non-archaeometrician archaeologist.

The definitional role of archaeometry referred to above is one in which archaeological scientists find it necessary and useful to depend upon the advice and wisdom of scientists in other professions. The information provided to archaeologists makes them consumers of information and most often archaeologists have no basis for independently evaluating that information. Another role is that of the non-archaeological scientist who must deal with a finite set of matter (i.e. the archaeological sample). Most often the archaeometrician is told that the implications of the analysis are enormous, that it will resolve some important question of eminent moment. However, the archaeometrician is now placed in the same position as the archaeologist evaluating archaeometric date. In most cases, the individual has no way to independently evaluate the dimensions of the archaeological problem. At the very minimum this kind of a situation demands extraordinary communication. It is at this level that we define archaeometry: the communication among two specialists, one an archaeologist, the other with substantial or complete training in another scientific discipline, that is directed toward the resolution of a particular set of issues pertinent to understanding some aspect of the past.

One of the major sources of misunderstanding between archaeologists and archaeometricians involves the way that particular analytical techniques are described or portrayed. The potential of some particular analytical technique, and its limitations, are well understood by the nonarchaeological scientist who undertakes a set of analyses. That same understanding is rarely shared by archaeologists. There is simply no way in which the application of archaeometry will be successful if the analytical strategies needed to resolve some problem are represented as proven analytical techniques when, in fact, they are still in the developmental stages. It is also the case that the non-archaeologist should never be told that a piece of information is secure if the interpretation is still surrounded by a substantial degree of conjecture.

One example of the kind of problem that we have been discussing concerns samples of material we recovered from a series of features of undefined function. Attributes of the features suggested their possible use as either kilns, smelters, or hornos. Some of the specimens were from the site of Nuvakwewtaqa (Chavez Pass) near Winslow, Arizona, while the others were from Hohokam sites near Phoenix, Arizona. All of the specimens in question had attributes suggesting possible by-products of metallurgy. A preliminary analysis of the Nuvakwewtaqa sample indicated that it contained at least traces of meteoric iron. Given that the pit from which the Nuvakwewtaqa specimen was taken had attributes of a smelter, and that the function of Hohokam hornos is poorly understood, it was postulated that the specimens might be slag. All of the specimens were sent for analysis using neutron activation.

No evidence that the specimens were, in fact, slag was developed. Given that no previous evidence of smelting was known from the area, this result was not necessarily surprising. What was surprising was that all of the specimens were identified as melted basalt. Nuvakwewtaqa does, in fact, sit on a basalt outcrop. However, the only nearby source of basalt in the case of the Hohokam sites consists of river cobbles from the Salt River. While burned basalt has been recovered from hearths and hornos in Hohokam sites, there is currently no example of a melted or partially melted specimen. Further, it is unreasonable to postulate that prehistoric inhabitants of the region were exchanging basalt, a conclusion that would have been necessary since the analyst identified the different specimens as chemically identical.

This example is discussed neither in an effect to embarrass the analyst in question nor to question the utility of such analyses in general. It does, however, suggest a problem. We were able to learn what the specimens were not, but were left with no understanding of what they were. Clearly, the initial information sent to the lab proved to be inadequate. However, the alternative interpretation was formulated without seeking additional information, information that would have precluded the conclusion that was reached. In other words, there was a failure to communicate the dimensions of the problem on the one hand, and a failure to communicate the basis of the analytical results on the other. In this case, the goal of integrating the diverse backgrounds of the scientists into a single research enterprise was simply not achieved.

A second problem concerns the disparity in the techniques used by different investigators in what are parallel if not identical circumstances. For years, pollen analyses have been based upon some sort of standardized counting procedures, although the specific number of observations utilized has varied. Petrographic analyses are, from our perspective, identical to palynological ones in relation to the problem of making observations about the content of individual slides. Yet, petrographic analyses, in the main, are not yet based on any sort of standardized counting procedure. In essence, the typical approach is either wholly subjective (i.e. the specimen is characterized by) or is a simple presence-absence summary.Clearly, if "point counts" are necessary for the proper interpretation of pollen, the same must be true of petrography. One can only wonder how much information has been lost or how much misinformation generated by the failure of petrographers to attend to the problems that palynologists have already resolved.

Ceramic Production and Distribution:
New Interpretations

While we have expressed a number of reservations concerning the manner in which petrography is done at present, we also wish to emphasize the very critical changes in our interpretation of prehistory that these studies can suggest. It should be clear from our previous comments that we recognize the need for a great deal of additional work in order to confirm or reject these interpretations. The example we will use is an analysis of petrographic characteristics of sherds from north-central Arizona that has been on-going for the last five years.

Two hundred forty six specimens collected from sites along a 240 km axis running through the Apache-Sitgreaves and Coconino National Forests have now been analyzed. The petrographic analysis was done by Elizabeth Garrett (1982). She utilized both point count and non-point count approaches in her effort. While we are currently preparing the point count results for computer analysis, we have completed preliminary analysis of the qualitative data and will discuss some preliminary conclusions. Garrett recorded over a dozen petrographic characteristics of each sherd. Some of these seem to vary in a random fashion among the sherds. Patterned variation, however, is characteristic of several attributes including the following: monocrystalline quartz (present/sparse, absent), polycrystalline quartz (sparse, absent), chert (present/absent), untwinned feldspar (present/absent), rock fragments (present/absent), and ferromanganese minerals (present/absent).

We sorted sherds into groups based upon these characteristics. For each ceramic type analyzed we attempted to identify a "core cluster" of sherds that were identical. In most instances, this task was a simple one. In a few cases, however, the cluster consisted of sherds that were similar but not identical. Additional sherds were added to each cluster if they differed from the characteristics of the core by only a single attribute.

This approach seems both reasonable and necessary. Given that sherds are made from naturally occurring clays, it seems highly probable that sherds made from the clays of a single source will occasionally have a particle that differs from the majority of sherds. Similarly, since many of the types analyzed contain sherd temper, the likelihood that different types of sherds were crushed to make the temper creates a high probability that an occasional rare particle will occur. For these reasons, we did not require that the sherds in a final cluster be identical, but only that they differ from the core definition by no more than a single attribute. In this manner we defined what might be called "temper types."

The number of temper types associated with each ceramic type used in this analysis is shown in Table 12.1. Not all types appear either because we do not yet have the full set of data or because the number of sherds for that type was too small to warrant analysis. Also shown in the table are the number of localities from which the sherds were taken and the number of sherds analyzed. The number of sherds analyzed defines the maximum number of temper types that could have resulted. These data allow an interesting analysis of ceramic production in the area.For generations, ceramic production has been interpreted using a model that assumed village level production. In essence, each settlement was supposed to have produced a distinguishable variety of a type. Given this assumption, one would expect that the number of temper types would be identical to the number of sites from which materials were recovered. Since we do not currently have data specifying the site from which each specimen was taken, we will use localities as a substitute. Given a model of local production of all types, one would expect to find at least as many temper types as localities from which the specimens were taken. If, on the other hand, more centralized production and widespread exchange was common, one would expect fewer temper types than localities.

Both expectations are met by some of the types analyzed. Pinedale Black-on-red, Showlow Black-on-red, Puerco Black-on-white and Red Mesa Black-on-white are types characterized by the maximum possible diversity—there are as many temper types as sherds. In these cases, the number of localities is irrelevant because the data suggest that with more specimens and/or localities, there would be more definable temper types. In any case, the number of temper types equals or exceeds the number of localities in every instance. Interestingly, the types in question are early Cibola White Wares and early White Mountain Redware types.

St. Johns Polychrome, Showlow Polychrome and Fourmile Polychrome are examples of types where the number of sherds does exceed the number of localities. In each of these three cases, the number of temper types equals or exceeds the number of localities. The Showlow Polychrome sherds do fall into two good clusters. Fourmile Polychrome is characterized by a single good cluster and great diversity in the remaining sherds. St. Johns Polychrome shows no significant clustering at all. Thus, a good case can be made for localized production in the case of all three of these types.

In the case of Pinedale Polychrome, Homolovi.Polychrome, Tuwiuca Black-on-orange, Reserve, Tularosa, Snowflake, Pinedale, Walnut and Black Mesa Black-on-white, there are fewer temper types than localities. Thus, at least some exchange from production centers is suggested. Homolovi Polychrome provides the most clearcut evidence for exchange. The sherds analyzed were from Nuvakwewtaqa, Chevelon Ruin, and Pinedale Ruin. The specimens form a tight cluster with only two sherds differing from the core group by a single attribute. Snowflake Black-on-white lies at the opposite extreme. With five potential production centers, production was certainly not localized, but sherds of this type do occur in areas where the type was apparently not being produced. Other types fall between these two extremes.

Current evidence supports the existence of both locally produced types and types that were produced at centers and exchanged over a widespread area. Clearly, the model of village level production can no longer be justified. However, it should not be replaced by a model of centralized production and widespread exchange. What was occurring during most periods lies somewhere in between. Given the presence of both patterns, additional questions concerning the process of ceramic production are generated. For example, early Cibola White Wares and early White Mountain Redwares are quite diverse suggesting localized production. Later examples of these wares suggest more centralization (cf. Graves 1978; Upham 1982). This may indicate that the two traditions began as the products of diverse settlements with one or a few settlements eventually becoming centers of production. The patterns of Homolovi Polychrome and Tuwiuca Black-on-orange suggest a very different pattern—great homogeneity is present from the outset. Investigation of these and related issues will certainly increase our understanding of the processes of ceramic production and exchange in the area.

We may summarize the implications of the current study as follows:

1. It is no longer tenable to assume that ceramic production occurred at most southwestern sites (see S. Plog 1980). Had this productive pattern

been most typical, one would expect a very high degree of variability in the petrographic characteristics of samples taken from spatially diverse sites. For the majority of types, the petrographic characteristics are strikingly similar over the entire area or within particular major localities. Other studies in the area demonstrate an even more homogeneous patterns for plainware ceramic types, a category of data that we did not investigate. While these relatively simpler types are certainly the best candidates for home manufacture, the diversity that should exist if the vessels were made in every or even most settlements is not present. Instead, the petrographic pattern is more consistent with the interpretation of plainware vessels as mass produced "tin cans."

2. The number of probable manufacturing centers varies markedly among the different types. The number of manufacturing centers for the different types most certainly varies through time as well. Consequently, reconstructing patterns of ceramic manufacture and distribution poses unusually complex problems for both the archaeologist and archaeo-metrician.

3. Even without the analysis of local clays, there appear to be local signatures that cross-cut different types. That is, when one examines those types for which multiple manufacturing centers are suggested, differences in the specimens from particular localities are evident; one can use the sorting procedure described above to identify spatial patterns that differentiate localities. Specimens from the Chavez Pass area, for example, tend to have high quantities of biotite, those from the Pinedale area high quantities of chert inclusions, and those from the Springerville area high quantities of igneous rock fragments. Thus, even without the analysis of local clays, a stratagem that will ultimately be necessary, it is possible to make general suggestions concerning the likely area of manufacture of different types of petrographically similar groups within types.

4. Similarities across space relate poorly to the cultural boundaries that have been proposed for the area. The most telling instance of this problem concerns the traditional distinction between Anasazi and Mo-gollon ceramics. Plog and Hantman (1982) and Hantman (1984) have described studies of specimens from Black Mesa, Arizona, in the Anasazi heartland, and the Apache-Sitgreaves Forests, central-eastern Arizona, a Mogollon area. The sherds from Black Mesa are very similar petro-graphically to sherds from the western end of the Forests. The sherds from the west Forests' area are more similar to the Black Mesa materials than to the sherds from the other "Mogollon" areas. Furthermore, there are marked spatial boundaries that can be identified among different localities on the forests on the basis of petrography. These boundaries are far sharper than any that can be drawn between the Mogollon and

Anasazi samples. The analyses in question were done using painted wares. It is unlikely that a similar circumstance would emerge if the grayware ceramics of the Anasazi were compared to the brownware ceramics of the Mogollon. However, the data clearly indicate the fallacy of using the brownware-grayware distinction as if it clearly differentiated culturally or ethnically different groups. A complex pattern of ceramic manufacture and distribution, probably associated with an equally complex pattern of culture, ethnicity, and/or social interaction is indicated.

One final comment needs to be made regarding our use of petrographic analysis. We are not sure even now, after a substantial investment of time and research dollars, that petrographic analysis is the appropriate technique to resolve problems of identifying manufacturing localities and patterns of local and regional exchange. We are sure, however, that after analyzing hundreds of sherds that our sample is simply too small. We believe that to resolve the questions we have raised we will require data on thousands of sherds from a number of different localities. It is important to emphasize that virtually all petrographic studies of ceramics, including our own, have relied on far too small a sample to be able to draw firm conclusions about the nature of constituent variability in pottery made at a particular locality, let alone across regions. Rather, the tentative conclusions we and others have offered should form the basis of hypotheses for future research. We should also emphasize that we are committed to continuing our petrographic analysis of ceramics from the montane and plateau regions of the Southwest. We feel it is important to determine if this particular technique can aid archaeologists in describing and explaining meaningful patterns of constituent variability in ceramics. In addition, we intend to begin the very important study of clay sources that are known in the area.

Conclusion

In this paper we have attempted to describe some of the problems we perceive with the uncritical use of archaeometric techniques. We have attempted to be balanced in our treatment of these issues, recognizing that when cooperative research endeavors involving scientists from diverse backgrounds go astray, they generally do so because of a failure to communicate. We believe that communication problems are perhaps the most difficult to come to grips with but, when recognized, can certainly be resolved. It is essential for archaeologists to be aware of such problems if archaeometry is to be successfully integrated into archaeological research.

We have also attempted to describe some of the useful knowledge that we have gained from the use of various archaeometric techniques.

While our experience with archaeometricians has involved periodic lapses of communication, there is no doubt that the data accumulated from such analyses have improved our understanding of the past. This fact may be among the most important of the statements we have made in this paper. In spite of the problems we have faced, and we believe they are problems shared by most archaeologists who use archaeometric techniques, our experiences have not been entirely negative. When we undertake discussions with scientists from other disciplines without making evident the assumptions that would underlie a similar discussion among archaeologists, we risk having interpretations of materials generated that do not meet archaeological expectations. There is no doubt that the archaeometrician can be of greater aid to the archaeologist if alternative hypotheses are identified and all of the expectations are made clear prior to initiating the intended research.

References Cited

Garrett, Elizabeth. "A Petrographic Analysis of Ceramics from the Apache-Sitgreaves National Forests, Arizona: On-site or Specialized Manufacture." Unpublished Ph.D. dissertation, Western Michigan University, Kalamazoo, 1982.

Graves, Michael. "White Mountain Redware Design Variability." Paper presented at the 77th Annual Meetings of the American Anthropological Association, Los Angeles, 1978.

Hantman, Jeffrey L. "Explaining Change in Regional Stylistic Distributions: A Behavioral Model." Unpublished Ph.D dissertation, Department of Anthropology, Arizona State University, Tempe, 1984.

Plog, Stephen. *Stylistic Variation in Prehistoric Ceramics: Design Analysis in the American Southwest.* Cambridge University Press, Cambridge, 1980.

Plog, Stephen, and Hantman, Jeffrey L. "Multiple Regression Analysis as a Dating Method in the American Southwest." Paper presented at the 47th Annual Meetings of the Society for American Archaeology, Tucson, Arizona, 1982.

Upham, Steadman. *Politics and Power: An Economic and Political History of the Western Pueblo.* Academic Press, New York, 1982.

Table 12.1
Summary of Petrographic Analysis

Pottery type	# Locations	# Sherds	# Temper Types Present
St. Johns Poly	7	16	8
St. Johns B/r	4	5	4
Pinedale B/r	1	2	2
Showlow B/r	1	3	3
Pinedale Poly	4	8	2
Fourmile Poly	4	12	5
Showlow Poly	2	8	2
Homolovi Poly	3	8	1
Tuwiuca B/o	3	16	2
Reserve B/w	7	18	3
Tularosa B/w	7	15	3
Snowflake B/w	7	18	5
Puerco B/w	1	4	4
Pinedale B/w	3	6	2
Red Mesa B/w	3	3	3
Walnut B/w	6	13	4
Black Mesa B/w	2	5	1

13

Tinkering with Technology: Pitfalls and Prospects for Anthropological Archaeology

Gary M. Feinman

Department of Anthropology,
University of Wisconsin–Madison

Well, son, I'll give you my opinion, said the Old Timer. I don't believe there's any such thing as 'archeological theory.' For me there's only *anthropological* theory. Archeologists have their own methodology, and ethnologists have theirs; but when it comes to theory, we all ought to sound like anthropologists. (Flannery 1982:269–270)

One of the most significant changes in archaeology over the last half century has been the increasing reliance on new analytical methods and scientific procedures (Wiseman 1980; Dyson 1985; Feinman 1987). Computers, carbon-14, aerial photographs, neutron activation, pollen analysis, petrography, and many other technological advances all have contributed dramatically to our current perspective on the past. The applicability of some of these new laboratory procedures to ceramic analysis is evident in this volume as well as in other recent works (e.g. Van der Leeuw and Pritchard ed. 1984).

Yet over the last decade, archaeology's increasing reliance on scientific and technological analyses seems to correspond with a diminished dialogue between the discipline and socio-cultural anthropology. Obviously, this decreasing communication also owes much to the increasing affinity for humanistic approaches in the latter field, as well as to the general demographic expansion (and to a degree, disintegration) of anthropology as whole. Nevertheless, archaeologists must bear part of the responsibility, for increasingly our debate is focused on our somewhat idiosyncratic methods rather than on interpretations of past human behaviors, a trend evident in Stephen L. Dyson's (1985) topical analysis of *American Antiquity* articles from 1935–84.

Despite the current disjuncture with certain branches of contemporary cultural anthropology, archaeology's roots and goals still lie in the social sciences, with questions concerning the emergence and explanation of cultural differences, similarities, and change. Hence, archaeological methods and techniques should not be elaborated, debated, and criticized in the abstract, but rather in a context that considers and evaluates the specific contributions made to our understanding of past human behaviors.

The works of Braun (1983) and Steponaitis (1984) have set a standard for the application of ceramic technology to the investigation of broader anthropological concerns, such as dietary change and production strategies. In this volume, Kaiser and Lucius's thermal expansion experiments on pottery strengthen the extant argument for the indigenous development of Balkan metallurgy. Reid's materials science approach has provided an interesting hypothesis for the use of clay vessels among the indigenous hunter-gatherers of northwestern North America, and Li Hu Hou's use of trace element analysis offers us a better understanding of the Song Dynasty palace economy.

One of the analytical themes in the works of Braun and Steponaitis, as well as in several of the papers in this volume (e.g. Wallace), is the increasing concern with technological efficiency or the relative function of specific ceramic attributes. In such analyses, variation in pottery composition or form are illustrated through experimental analyses to have different functional attributes. Shifts or diversity in these characteristics are then interpreted as related to changing strategies of production, distribution, consumption or use. While the interpretation of change towards increasing efficiency in craft items has been shown to be a productive analytical tact (and makes a certain amount of intuitive sense), we must remember that a durable ceramic product (resistant to thermal and/or mechanical stresses) is not always in the best interest of the specialist potter. General Electric could make a reasonably-priced lightbulb that lasts almost indefinitely, but they do not. Likewise, ceramic specialists may have an interest in eventually exchanging or selling more pots. Even consumers of craft products often weigh aesthetic attributes ahead of relatively minor differences in durability or efficiency.

Even when increasing technological efficiency has been shown to be a key factor in ceramic change, relatively few studies have grappled with the questions of why did change occur in the specific way that it did or why did shifts happen at the precise times that they did. Often there seems to be tacit acceptance of simple innovation-diffusion models. Yet, such models have not proven very convincing for the spread of farming (e.g. Price 1987:285), nor can they explain the checkered distribution and occasional abandonment of the potter's wheel in Europe and North Africa (e.g. Balfet 1965, Van der Waals 1965). If we are to understand ceramic change, we must examine it in a broad cultural context that enables us both to consider the pre-existing pottery tradition as well as the numerous factors (e.g. transport, resource availability, demography, shifting boundaries, cooking considerations, socio-political relations) that may prompt a transition (see Rice 1984).

I have structured my discussion in this cautionary manner, not so much as a result of new concerns, but rather because we need to encourage a more holistic approach to ceramic analysis (one that includes consideration of technological attributes, but not at the exclusion of other factors). In addition, our technological studies (of pottery as well as other materials) should be designed with broad anthropological issues in mind (see Upham and Plog, this volume). Too frequently in our journals, the focus is on new technical gadgetry rather than the interpretation of the past.

Continual reminders against such pitfalls are justified because of the strong influences which seem to pull all of us in the opposite direction. As Paul Connolly (1928:48) recently noted:

There is something myopic—and quintessentially American—about this fascination with . . . technology. Riddles, puzzles, colored cubes all whet our competitive urge to solve problems. But, life's darker mysteries make us impatient and anxious.

To a degree, the North American consumption with technology colors our research even in anthropology. Furthermore, in archaeology, where we frequently collaborate with 'hard' scientists, the problem may be exacerbated by feelings of inferiority regarding the nature of our data and the lack of theoretical consensus. At times, this may lead us to gather what appears to be hard, objective sets of data that are satisfying and straightforward to collect, but perhaps are not theoretically or anthropologically very relevant. On occasion, we have utilized models that are simply too mechanical and elementary to help us explain the complex human systems that we want to understand. We also face the problem that working to resolve broader, more holistic questions requires longer-term projects, more complex research designs, less immediate gratification, and usually somewhat more interpretive ambiguity.

In sum, we must continue to develop this very healthy interst in the technological and functional attributes of ceramic vessels. In addition, we must experiment with and refine new techniques of pottery analysis. But in so doing, we should strive to frame our research questions with the key issues of anthropology and the social sciences in mind.

References Cited

Balfet, Hélène. "Ethnographical Observations in North Africa and Archaeological Interpretation." in *Ceramics and Man*, edited by Frederick R. Matson. Viking Fund Publications in Anthropology 41:161–177, 1965.

Braun, David P. "Pots as Tools." in *Archaeological Hammers and Theories*, edited by A. Keene and J. Moore. New York: Academic Press, pp. 107–134, 1983.

Connolly, Paul. "Our Fascination with Electronic Technology is Myopic—and Quintessentially American." *The Chronical of Higher Education.* 25(4):48, September 22, 1982.

Dyson, Stephen L. "Two Paths to the Past: A Comparative Study of the Last Fifty Years of *American Antiquity* and the *American Journal of Archaeology.*" *American Antiquity* 50(2):452–463, 1985.

Feinman, Gary. "The Past is our Future: A Perspective on Contemporary Archaeology." *Wisconsin Academy Review.* 33(2):2–5, 1987.

Flannery, Kent V. "The Golden Marshalltown: A Parable for the Archaeology of the 1980s." *American Anthropologist* 84(2):265–278, 1982.

Price, T. Douglas. "The Mesolithic of Western Europe." *Journal of World Prehistory.* 1(3):225–305, 1987.

Rice, Prudence M. "Change and Conservatism in Pottery-Producing Systems." in *The Many Dimensions of Pottery: Ceramics in Archaeology and Anthropology*, edited by S.D. van der Leeuw and A.C. Pritchard. Amsterdam: Universiteit van Amsterdam, pp. 231–288, 1984.

Steponaitis, Vincas P. "Technological Studies of Prehistoric Pottery from Alabama: Physical Properties and Vessel Function." in *The Many Dimensions of Pottery: Ceramics in Archaeology and Anthropology*, edited by S.D. van der Leeuw and A.C. Pritchard. Amsterdam: Universiteit van Amsterdam, pp. 79–122, 1984.

van der Leeuw, Sander E., and Pritchard, Alison C. *The Many Dimensions of Pottery: Ceramics in Archaeology and Anthropology.* Amsterdam: Universiteit van Amsterdam, 1984.

Van der Waals, J.D. "Early Ceramics in the Netherlands: Two Problems." in *Ceramics and Man*, edited by Frederick R. Matson. Viking Fund Publications in Anthropology 41:124–139, 1965.

Wiseman, James. "Archaeology in the Future: An Evolving Discipline." *American Journal of Archaeology* 84:279– 285, 1980.